This book is a contribution to comparative constitutional law and deals with important changes in the United Kingdom, Canada, Australia, and New Zealand, the original members of the present Commonwealth of Nations. It is based on lectures delivered at the University of Cambridge under the auspices of the Smuts Memorial Fund.

The first lecture discusses the development in recent years of the constitutional autonomy of Canada, Australia, and New Zealand, and its effect on the Constitutions of those countries and on the concept of the 'crown'.

The second lecture is concerned with methods to entrench, constitutionally, individual and democratic rights. It examines the effect in Britain of adherence to the European Convention on Human Rights, the nature and judicial interpretation of the Canadian Charter of Rights and Freedoms, and proposals for bills of rights in Britain, Australia, and New Zealand. There is criticism of attempts by some Commonwealth judges to impose restrictions on parliamentary power in favour of individual rights in the absence of any specific constitutional provisions to that effect.

The final lecture contrasts judicial attitudes to the interpretation of the Constitutions of Canada and Australia. The position of Britain in relation to the European Economic Community is compared with the federal features of Canada and Australia. The conclusion is reached that, although the EEC is not a federation, there is a structural similarity between the distribution of governmental power within the Community and its members, and the federal issues that arise in Canada, Australia, and other federations.

CONSTITUTIONAL CHANGE IN
THE COMMONWEALTH

THE COMMONWEALTH LECTURES

DELIVERED AT THE UNIVERSITY OF CAMBRIDGE

ON 8, 15, AND 22 NOVEMBER 1988

CONSTITUTIONAL CHANGE IN THE COMMONWEALTH

LESLIE ZINES
Robert Garran Professor of Law, Australian National University

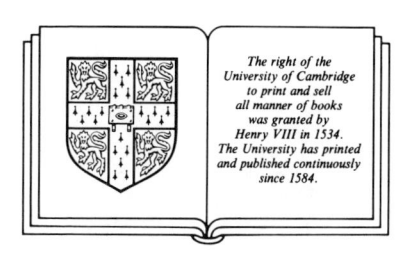

CAMBRIDGE UNIVERSITY PRESS
CAMBRIDGE
NEW YORK   PORT CHESTER   MELBOURNE   SYDNEY

Published by the Press Syndicate of the University of Cambridge
The Pitt Building, Trumpington Street, Cambridge CB2 1RP
40 West 20th Street, New York, NY 10011, USA
10 Stamford Road, Oakleigh, Melbourne 3166, Australia

© Cambridge University Press 1991

First published 1991

Printed in Great Britain at the University Press Cambridge

British Library cataloguing in publication data
Zines, Leslie, *1930* –
Constitutional change in the commonwealth.
1. Commonwealth countries. Constitutional law
I. Title
342.209171241

Library of Congress cataloguing in publication data
Zines, Leslie.
Constitutional change in the Commonwealth: the Commonwealth lectures delivered at the University of Cambridge on 8, 15 and 22 November 1988 / Leslie Zines.
p. cm.
ISBN 0 521 40039 2
1. Commonwealth of Nations – Constitutional law. I. University of Cambridge. II. Title. III. Title: Commonwealth lectures.
K3165.Z9Z56 1991
342′.03′09171241–dc20
[342.2309171241] 90-43071 CIP

ISBN 0 521 40039 2 hardback

CONTENTS

1 Constitutional autonomy — *page* 1
2 The entrenchment of individual and democratic rights — 33
3 Federal and supra-national features — 75

Index — 113

I

CONSTITUTIONAL AUTONOMY

This chapter is concerned with steps taken by Canada, Australia, and New Zealand, successfully completed only in the last few years, to end their constitutional ties with the United Kingdom Parliament and Government, to examine the present legal foundations of the Constitutions of those countries, and to see what has happened to the notion of 'the Crown'.

In Canada, Australia, and New Zealand, many academics in fields of law, politics, and history have had difficulty in answering a frequently asked question from foreign scholars: 'When did your country obtain its independence from Britain?' At times the courts have also adverted to that question and have been just as perplexed. The difficulty is that, unlike the case with other Commonwealth countries, one cannot point to an occasion when one flag was lowered and another raised at midnight amid sentiments of joy and nostalgia.

In a desperate effort to find some exact date for the event, the Balfour Declaration of 1926 or the Statute of Westminster of 1931 are seized on as roughly approximating independence days. Yet in 1939 and 1940 the Governments of Australia and New Zealand assumed that they were automatically at war with Germany and Italy when Britain was at war. Amendments to the *British North America Act* were made by, and could only be made by, the United Kingdom Parliament at various times up to and including 1982. A British parliamentary committee in 1981 and 1982 said that the British Government had an element of discretion or judgement in deciding whether to accede to a federal Canadian request for amendment.[1] It was accepted in 1979 that laws of the Australian States were invalid if they were inconsistent with Imperial legislation.[2] In 1974, it seems that the British Government refused to recommend an extension of the term of a Queensland Governor, opposed by the Commonwealth but desired by the Government of that State. While it was possible for constitutional lawyers and others to reconcile at least some of these facts with national independence, it caused confusion and bewilderment to others, particularly outsiders.

The evolutionary manner in which the independence of these countries was achieved in fact left many legal problems in its wake and, to some degree, still does. In order to understand what has happened in the last few years, it is necessary to traverse briefly some well-trodden ground.

Part of the difficulty has been caused by the fact that the Empire and then the British Commonwealth of Nations had few legal principles or rules that reflected political reality. The growth in status of the older Dominions was achieved

---

[1] First Report from the Foreign Affairs Committee Session 1980–1, British North America Acts: The Role of Parliament, House of Commons, 30 January 1981.

[2] *China Ocean Shipping Co. v South Australia* (1979) 145 Commonwealth Law Reports 172.

mainly, not by changes in law or alterations to the Constitutions of those countries, but by the development of constitutional conventions and understandings, particularly the convention as to who advises something called 'the Crown'.

In law all four countries were originally part of one system, subject to an indivisible Imperial Crown and an omnipotent Imperial Parliament. The Constitutions of Canada, the Commonwealth of Australia, the Australian States, and New Zealand derived from enactments of that Parliament. Their status as law depended upon a grundnorm requiring obedience to that Parliament. Judicial review of the legislation of a Dominion Parliament followed, on this view, as inevitably and naturally as review of any legislation authorized by an enactment. Thus Professor A. V. Dicey in his famous work *The Law and the Constitution* was able to place in the same category labelled 'non-sovereign legislatures' the Dominion of Canada, a London county council, and a railway company.[3]

The other feature of the system was the one indivisible Crown in which was reposed all the royal prerogatives. With few exceptions,[4] these prerogative powers operated throughout the Empire. What was not clear, either in the Constitutions or in the Royal Instructions, was which of them could in the overseas Dominions be exercised locally, that is by the Governor on the advice of local ministers. On

---

[3] A. V. Dicey (1959) *The Law and the Constitution*, 10th edn., Macmillan, London, chapter 11.

[4] Local circumstances could exclude or modify the application of a prerogative. This was the case with the prerogatives of the Sovereign as head of the established church.

this subject all British laws and instruments were, during this period, obstinately silent.[5]

The courts also shied away from laying down any general principles to distinguish those executive powers which were Imperial and those which were local. The matter was handled, by and large, administratively. A vice-regal representative had two capacities – Imperial officer subject to direction from the Crown, that is a British minister, and local representative of the Queen instructed to act on the advice of local ministers. While normally required to accept the advice of local ministers, the Governor was also required to ensure that matters of Imperial concern were not impaired by local legislative or executive action.

In retrospect it was perhaps fortunate that no clear dividing line between Imperial and local responsibility was devised. This imprecision enabled more and more executive power to be transferred to the Dominions, without any alteration to constitutional law, by simply changing the rule or understanding as to who advises the Crown.

The Constitutions were also broad enough in language for the courts to assume that the legislative powers of the Dominions conformed with whatever were the political understandings of the time as to the status of those Dominions. The judges were prepared to have regard to political changes in interpreting the Constitutions. A good example is a decision of the Privy Council in 1947 upholding the power of the Canadian Parliament to abolish appeals to the Privy

---

[5] On 1 October 1947 the King, by Letters Patent, authorized the Governor-General of Canada to 'exercise all powers and authorities lawfully belonging to Us in respect of Canada...': N. Mansergh (1953) *Documents and Speeches on British Commonwealth Affairs* (1931–52), Vol. 1, Oxford University Press, 78–81.

Council from any Canadian court.[6] The relevant provision was section 101 of the *British North America Act* which gave power to 'provide for the constitution, maintenance and organization of a general Court of Appeal for Canada ...'. Their Lordships declared that it was irrelevant that when section 101 was enacted it would have been unthinkable that Canada should have the power to abolish the prerogative appeal. To deny the power in 1947 would, they said, be inconsistent with the political conception embodied in the British Commonwealth. The Constitution had to be given the interpretation 'which changing circumstances require'.

The only relevant formal legal changes to the powers of the Dominions were made by the Statute of Westminster. That Statute achieved one important result. It enabled the Dominions to override Imperial law. For the rest it achieved little that was not merely symbolic. Empowering the Dominions to give extra-territorial effect to their laws was probably unnecessary.[7] Requiring the request and consent of the Dominion to Imperial legislation operating in the Dominion was already an established rule. Issues of war and peace and succession to the throne were fudged.

For the most part, therefore, it was conventions and practices, embodied partly in Conference resolutions, and international recognition, rather than the creation of judicially enforceable legal rules, that created the sovereign status in the world of Canada, Australia, and New Zealand. Although their Constitutions originated as governmental frameworks of self-governing colonies of an Empire, their international and political independence was brought about

---

[6] *Attorney-General (Ont) v Attorney-General (Can)* [1947] Appeal Cases 127.
[7] *New South Wales v Commonwealth* (1975) 135 Commonwealth Law Reports 337; *Union Steamship Co. of Australia Pty Ltd v King* (1988) 82 Australian Law Reports 43.

without any amendment being made to those Constitutions in order to achieve that end.

R. T. E. Latham, writing in 1937, put it this way:

When the political institutions of the colonies were first set up ... their constitutions were not intended to be the framework of a generally competent political organism, but only to exercise certain select powers. But those institutions became in fact political frameworks for nations, the reality of whose nationhood transcended the institutions of their origin.[8]

When, for example, section 61 of the Australian Constitution declared that the executive power of the Commonwealth was exercisable by the Governor-General, no judge at the time it was enacted would have considered that it included the power to declare war or to enter into treaties. Decades later it could be assumed without argument that such Commonwealth power existed. Yet the wording of section 61 had not changed.[9]

Similarly, the Canadian and Australian Constitutions, for example, give power to the Queen personally to appoint Governors-General. Those provisions have not been altered since they were first enacted in 1867 and 1900, respectively. Their operation today is, however, very different from when they were enacted. But from a constitutional point of view, all that has been altered are the Queen's advisers.

The federal Government of Canada (together with those of Ireland and South Africa), in the 1920s and 1930s, pressed strongly for these developments towards greater Dominion autonomy. Australia and New Zealand were dragged along

[8] R. T. E. Latham (1949) *The Law and the Commonwealth* Oxford University Press, London, 579.

[9] G. Winterton (1983) *Parliament, the Executive and the Governor-General*, Melbourne University Press, Chapter 1; L. Zines (1987), *The High Court and the Constitution*, 2nd edn, Butterworths, Australia, 224–5, 244–5.

on their coat-tails. They were cautious, suspicious, and at times alarmed at attempts to define by clear convention or legal rules the relationship between members of the Commonwealth. Their defence and trading interests, as well as the sentiments of their people, no doubt were responsible for this attitude.[10]

They, together with Newfoundland, insisted on a provision in section 10 of the Statute of Westminster that the major parts of the Act should not extend to them unless adopted by their Parliaments. Australia waited eleven years and New Zealand sixteen years before they adopted the Statute in 1942 and 1947 respectively.[11] In the meantime the United Kingdom Parliament had enacted laws extending to those countries at their request.[12]

It was thought necessary in the case of both Canada and Australia expressly to ensure that nothing in the Statute of Westminster would affect the federal systems of those countries (sections 7 and 8). New Zealand, perhaps not wanting to appear more radical, but with no federal system to defend, was also included in section 8 which saved the Constitutions of all three countries.

In Australia, there was an added level of suspicion and concern – that of the States in respect of the federal Government. The States of Australia (unlike the Canadian Provinces) had attended the Colonial Conferences of 1887 and 1897, but then found themselves shut out after fede-

---

[10] F. Scott (1933) *Cambridge History of the British Empire*, Vol. 7, Pt 1, Cambridge University Press, 542.

[11] *The Statute of Westminster Adoption Act 1942* (Cth) adopted the Statute from 3 September 1939.

[12] For example, *Whaling Industry (Regulation) Act 1934, Emergency; Powers (Defence) Act 1939, Prize Act 1939, Army and Air Force (Annual) Act 1940, Geneva Convention Act 1937*.

ration, despite vigorous protests and energetic attempts to obtain admission to the 1907 Conference. They were concerned that any increase in the autonomy of the Dominions should not take place at their expense. Also, they did not want the Commonwealth Government interfering in their relations with the United Kingdom Government.[13]

Unlike the Canadian Provinces, the States of Australia had direct communication with the British Government on all matters within their authority. The British Government therefore played a larger part in Australian State affairs than in those of the Canadian Provinces. The appointment of State Governors, their instructions, and the reservation and disallowance of State legislation were British responsibilities. In Canada it was the federal Government which exercised those functions in respect of the Provinces. Before federation the Australian colonies were quite scornful of the position of the Canadian Provinces. For example, delegates to the Constitutional Convention of 1891 resoundingly rejected a proposal of the chief architect of the Constitution (Sir Samuel Griffith) that all communications between the States and the British Government should be sent through the Governor-General. The States, they insisted, must have equal status with the Commonwealth on all matters within their governmental responsibilities, including communication with the Home Government.[14]

The States feared that section 4 of the Statute of Westminster providing for the request and consent of a Dominion to the enactment of United Kingdom legislation applying to the Dominion could result in the central Government med-

[13] L. Zines, 'The Growth of Australian Nationhood and Its Effect on the Powers of the Commonwealth', In L. Zines (ed.) (1977) *Commentaries on the Australian Constitution*, Butterworths, Australia, 24.
[14] *Ibid.*, 16–20.

dling in their sphere of responsibility. There was, therefore, introduced into the Statute section 9(2) which declared that nothing was deemed to require the concurrence of the federal authorities to any United Kingdom law with respect to a matter solely within State authority. The States actually wished to go further and prevent the federal Government from requesting or consenting to such legislation. The British claimed that would be achieved by section 9(2), but that clearly was not the case because, while section 9(2) prevented any suggestion that Commonwealth consent was required in this area, the amendment requested by the States would have prevented the Commonwealth from making any submissions.[15]

What is clear is that the States trusted the British Government more than they did the federal Government, which they saw, quite rightly, as a competitor for power. The Imperial tie was regarded as some protection for States rights. I should mention, tangentially, that it proved unavailing on the only occasion when a State attempted to secede from the Australian Commonwealth. As a result of a referendum in 1933, two-thirds of the electorate of Western Australia voted in favour of secession from the Australian Commonwealth. A delegation was sent to Britain to request an amendment to the *Commonwealth of Australia Constitution Act* to achieve that result. This action was opposed by the federal Government, and a Joint Committee of the House of Lords and the House of Commons advised that the petition should not be received unless supported by that Government.[16]

The result of this internecine political fighting within

---

[15] *Ibid.*, 30.
[16] 1934–5 *Parliamentary Papers*, Vol. 11, 63.

Australia was that the States did not seek to have applied to them the substantive provisions of the Statute of Westminster. On the other hand, the Canadian Provinces were freed from the *Colonial Laws Validity Act* and expressly empowered to make laws overriding Imperial laws. Neither did the States acquire (nor, I think, seek) the power given to the Dominion Governments to advise the Queen directly on matters within their authority. The Secretary of State still ruled. From 1934 to 1947 Western Australia had no Governor because the British Government refused to recommend the appointment of an Australian, as desired by the Government of that State.[17]

The consequent difference in status between the federal and State Governments of Australia gave rise to many constitutional and legal conundrums. Whereas relations between the British and Australian Governments came to be primarily on an international and diplomatic level, the States in their relations with Britain retained all the elements of colonial status. Until 1986 it was the British Government which formally advised the Queen of the United Kingdom on such matters as the appointment of State Governors or the making of orders or proclamations relating to the States under Imperial legislation. As section 2 of the Statute of Westminster did not extend to the States, they could not amend or repeal legislation such as the *Merchant Shipping Act* which applied to them.

To make matters worse, modern amendments by the British Parliament to former Imperial legislation were not extended to the States, so that it was the legislation as enacted around the turn of the century that applied, rather

---

[17] J. Fajgenbaum and P. Hanks (1972) *Australian Constitutional Law*, Butterworths, Australia, 20.

than the legislation in its modern British form.[18] Similarly, it seemed that the States could not abolish appeals to the Privy Council from judgements of State courts.[19]

By federal legislation enacted in 1968 and 1975, appeals to the Privy Council ceased from the High Court of Australia, federal and territorial courts, and all State courts exercising federal jurisdiction.[20] Appeals from State courts exercising State jurisdiction continued. The States differed among themselves as to whether such appeals should be abolished. In the meantime, the High Court had indicated that it did not regard itself as bound by Privy Council decisions. As it was possible in many cases to appeal from a State court in a matter arising under State law to *either* the High Court *or* the Privy Council, the system of precedent threatened to become chaotic. The High Court of Australia found it could not give the State courts guidance as to what they should do where prior High Court and Privy Council judgements differed.[21]

Federal Governments from the early 1970s onwards became anxious to clear up this situation and that of the status of the States generally, which was seen as an affront to Australian national sentiment as well as legally absurd. As late as 1981 a Foreign and Commonwealth Office memorandum to the Foreign Affairs Committee of the House of Commons was able to describe the States of Australia as 'self-governing dependencies of the British Crown'.[22]

[18] *Copyright Owners Reproduction Society Ltd v EMI (Aust.) Pty* (1958) 100 Commonwealth Law Reports 597.
[19] *Nadan v R* [1926] Appeal Cases 482; *British Coal Corporation v R* [1935] Appeal Cases 500; but see *Commonwealth v Queensland* (1975) 134 Commonwealth Law Reports 298 at 311–12.
[20] *Privy Council (Limitation of Appeals) Act 1968* (Cth); *Privy Council (Appeals from the High Court) Act 1975* (Cth).
[21] *Viro v R* (1978) 141 Commonwealth Law Reports 88.
[22] G. Marshall (1984) *Constitutional Conventions*, Clarendon, Oxford, 173.

To some degree, the Australians may have been spurred on by events in Canada, where Provincial concerns also acted as a preserver of the Imperial bond. Whereas the Australian Constitution contained a provision for local amendment (section 128), the *British North America Act* did not, except to a limited extent.

As I mentioned earlier, section 7 of the Statute of Westminster saved from the operation of that Statute the alteration or repeal of the *British North American Act*. Most of the provisions of the *British North America Act* could, therefore, be legally altered only by the United Kingdom Parliament. It was, of course, a clearly expressed rule that Parliament would make no law for Canada except at the request and with the consent of Canada. To that extent, as a matter of practical reality, this situation did not derogate from Canada's independence.

But the conventional rule did not make it clear what 'Canada' was or how its request and consent was to be expressed. Was it sufficient for the British Parliament to enact legislation if the request had been made simply by both Houses of the federal Parliament? Should the British Government inquire as to the agreement of the Provinces? If so, must all the Governments, or, possibly, legislatures of the Provinces affected agree, or only a majority of them, or nearly all of them? Although all amendments to the *British North America Act* from 1895 had arisen out of joint addresses of the Canadian House of Commons and Senate, constitutional practice regarding the consent of the Provinces was not clear.[23]

Attempts to obtain an agreement on an amending for-

[23] P. W. Hogg (1985) *Constitutional Law of Canada*, 2nd edn, Carswell, Toronto, 52–3.

mula were made at federal–Provincial Conferences on many occasions between 1927 and 1979. They all failed. The Prime Minister of Canada, Mr Trudeau, declared in 1981 that, if Provincial consent could not be obtained to certain proposed alterations to the *British North America Act* (including an amending process and a Charter of Rights), the federal Government would, after a resolution of both Houses of the Canadian Parliament, unilaterally request a British enactment.

This caused some fluttering in the dovecotes in Whitehall and in the United Kingdom Houses of Parliament, as well as in Canada. Was it for Britain to lay down the rules and refuse a federal request? Had the old notion of trustee for the Empire survived to a degree so as to impose fiduciary obligations on Britain to protect Canadian federalism? A Committee of the House of Commons – known as the Kershaw Committee – proceeded in 1981 to examine and report on the question.

The Canadian Government refused to give evidence to the Committee, considering it 'inappropriate for the executive government of one nation to offer advice to a committee of the Parliament of another nation'. The Committee however declared that the Parliament should only comply with the Canadian request for amendment if there was *in the view of that Parliament* 'a sufficient level and distribution of provincial concurrence'. This differed from the view expressed by the Canadian Government and by Laskin CJ at the Australian National University five years before, that any attempt by the British Government or Parliament to go behind a resolution of the federal Houses would be strongly resented and could lead to the departure of Canada from the Commonwealth. However that may be, it could obviously have led to great diplomatic conflict between the two countries. It should be mentioned that the position taken by the Kershaw Committee was not necessarily that of the British Government.[24]

In the end, no conflict eventuated, partly as a result of unusual action by the Supreme Court of Canada. After Mr Trudeau made his threat of unilateral request, a number of Provinces commenced suits for advisory judgements which reached that Court. The Supreme Court affirmed the legal power of the Canadian Houses to pass the appropriate resolutions and declared that the Parliament at Westminster was legally 'untrammelled' and 'omnipotent' in relation to Canada.

A majority, then, answered questions that related not to law but to constitutional convention. They said that there was a constitutional convention requiring the agreement of the Provinces to a federal petition to Britain for the kind of constitutional alteration that was proposed. They expressly refrained from comment on, or advice to, the British Government and Parliament. The convention, they held, required a 'substantial' degree or measure of Provincial consent, but not necessarily unanimity.[25]

In the upshot only Quebec dissented from the proposals, which differed in a number of respects from those that had been before the Court. The Supreme Court of Canada held later that there could be a substantial degree of Provincial consent, for purposes of the convention, without the consent of Quebec.[26] The British Parliamentary Committee agreed,

---

[24] P. W. Hogg, Comment (1982) 60 *Canadian Bar Review* 307–34.
[25] *Reference re Amendment of the Constitution of Canada* (1982) 125 Dominion Law Reports (3d) 1.
[26] *Re Objection by Quebec to Resolution to Amend the Constitution* [1982] 2 Supreme Court Reports 793.

and that Parliament enacted, as its last law operating in Canada, the *Canada Act* 1982.

This legislation provided, among other things, for local amendment of the Constitution of Canada and for a *Canadian Charter of Rights and Freedoms*. It further provided that no Act of Parliament of the United Kingdom would henceforth extend to Canada as part of its law. Consequently, section 4 of the Statute of Westminster (the request and consent provision) was repealed in relation to Canada.

In the meantime, in Australia, the federal Government was having difficulty getting the States to agree on the method of getting rid of their colonial restrictions and their dependence on the United Kingdom authorities. One problem was the issue of advice to the Queen. It was said that the Queen, herself, did not relish the idea of being advised directly by State Governments. The Commonwealth Government also considered that, as it was the national Government, any advice to the Queen of Australia should be channelled through it. The States strongly resisted. When the Whitlam Government attempted to persuade the British Goverment to take unilateral action regarding such matters as Privy Council appeals, the Australian States, in 1973, addressed a memorandum to that Government as follows:

The Government and Parliament of the United Kingdom are constitutionally bound to consider the wishes of the Governments of the States when faced with requests by the Commonwealth upon a matter which is primarily one of concern to the States.[27]

One problem was that of the possibility of the Queen receiving conflicting advice, with each Government claiming that it was the appropriate Government to give the effective advice.

[27] G. Marshall (1984) *Constitutional Conventions* Clarendon, Oxford, 189.

This spectre of differing advice from Governments in a federation in the somewhat cloudy area of constitutional law and practice was raised in connection with requests by the Queensland and Tasmanian Governments to the British Government in 1973 to advise the Queen to refer to the Judicial Committee of the Privy Council, under section 4 of the *Judicial Committee Act* 1833, a question related to the ownership of and dominion over the territorial sea and seabed adjacent to Queensland and Tasmania. This occurred three weeks after the introduction into the federal Parliament of the *Seas and Submerged Lands Bill*, which, among other things, declared that sovereignty over the territorial sea and seabed was vested in the Commonwealth. The validity of this legislation depended, in part, on whether the territorial sea was part of the territory of each of the States. When the federal Government heard of the States' requests, it advised against such a reference on the ground that it was properly a matter for the High Court of Australia. The British Government also advised against the reference.

The State Governments concerned were informed by the Foreign and Commonwealth Office that the Queen had acted on the advice of the British Government. The Governor-General sent letters to the two State Governors stating that the Queen had acted on the advice of the Australian Government that the petitions should be rejected on the grounds that the High Court of Australia was the appropriate tribunal to determine the issues.[28] In referring to this matter in her speech to the Australian Parliament on 28 February 1974, embarrassment was avoided by the Govern-

---

[28] Dispute as to the significance of these events is referred to in correspondence in the *Australian Law Journal* (1981) 55 *Australian Law Journal* at 360, 701, 763, 829, 893. See also Harders (1982) 56 *Australian Law Journal* 132.

ment recording in her speech that she had acted on the advice of 'My Australian and United Kingdom Ministers'.[29] This posed the question of what would have happened had the two advices conflicted.

Questions of this sort also produced an argument that has been made in both Canada and Australia as to the propriety of British Governments consulting or considering the wishes of the regional Governments of those countries since they became independent States in international law. The Whitlam Government had at times suggested that, as the relationship of the Australian Government and the United Kingdom Government was an international and diplomatic one, rather than an Imperial and constitutional one, the British Government had no business going behind the federal Government to concern itself with the municipal organization of the country. The federal Government spoke for the whole of Australia in international affairs and at international law. The internal organization of government and the distribution of power within the country were of no concern to other countries, and that included Britain.

This argument was also made by the federal Government of Canada in protest against the view of the Kershaw Committee that it was for the British Government to satisfy itself that there was sufficient Provincial support for the proposed amendments to the *British North America Act*. The British Government, it was argued, should deal only with the Canadian Government, as it does in ordinary international affairs, and not seek the views of the internal governmental units. A background paper prepared by the Canadian

---

[29] Commonwealth Parliament Debates, House of Representatives, Vol. 88, 6.

Department of Justice attacked the Kershaw Report as constituting an interference in Canadian internal affairs.[30]

Whatever might be said of this reasoning from the point of view of constitutional and international propriety, it provided the seeds of a *legal* argument that the Australian Government had the constitutional power to deliver the States from colonial bondage, without the intervention of the British Parliament and Government. Indeed, once the States had generally come round to the idea of legal independence from Britain, one of the main arguments was whether, or the extent to which, British intervention was necessary or desirable.

One device considered was the power in the federal Parliament to make laws with respect to 'external affairs'. The subject matter of that power is concerned primarily with relations between Australia and other countries. Once relations between Australia and Britain became international as a result of independence, it was possible to argue that it was valid under the external affairs power to enact a federal law which was designed to prevent the application within Australia of laws of the Parliament of another country, that is, the United Kingdom, or actions of the Queen of the United Kingdom, that is, taken on the advice of British Ministers, or to prevent appeals to the courts in another country, namely the Privy Council. On this view, there could be no clearer example of a law relating to external affairs than one which ensured that the governmental authorities of another country could not interfere with Australia's domestic affairs. For this purpose, the quasi-colonial status of the States could not affect the fact that relations between Australia and the United Kingdom on the

[30] *The Role of the United Kingdom in the Amendment of the Canadian Constitution*, Department of Justice (1981) 37–8, Queen's Printer, Ottawa.

international scene were those between sovereign nations.

This issue came before the High Court of Australia in 1985, but was not fully resolved. Mrs Kirmani, while enjoying a cruise on Sydney Harbour, on a ferry operated by Captain Cook Cruises Pty Ltd, suffered injury as a result of the negligence of the company's servants. The company admitted liability, but pleaded that the damages were limited as a result of the provisions of the (Imperial) *Merchant Shipping Act* 1894. Mrs Kirmani, however, replied that the particular provision had been repealed by the federal Parliament in 1979. It was assumed that this provision was not authorized by the ordinary constitutional powers of the federal Parliament. The ousting of the Imperial law was designed to enable the States to legislate free of the overriding effect of the Imperial law. The Commonwealth argued that its law was valid under its power over external affairs, as it dealt with relations with another country.

It was held valid by four judges to three (Mason, Murphy, Brennan, and Deane JJ; Gibbs CJ, Wilson, and Dawson JJ dissenting).[31] However, only six of the seven judges (all except Brennan J) discussed the external affairs power, and they were evenly split. Three of the majority judges held that to prevent British law operating in Australia was a matter of external affairs, involving, as it did, relations with another country. The other three judges said the matter related to the internal law of the States. Even one of the minority judges, Gibbs, CJ, however, conceded that the *future* exercise by the United Kingdom Parliament of its powers in relation to Australia might be described as 'an external affair'.

The other federal power that became relevant is one that has caused puzzlement from the beginning of federation. It is

[31] *Kirmani v Captain Cook Cruises Pty Ltd [No. 1]* (1985) 159 Commonwealth Law Reports 351.

section 51 (xxxviii), which provides (so far as relevant) that the Parliament has power 'subject to this Constitution' to make laws with respect to:

The exercise, within the Commonwealth, at the request or with the concurrence of the Parliaments of all the States directly concerned, of any power which can at the establishment of this Constitution be exercised only by the Parliament of the United Kingdom ...

It is unnecessary, here, to go into all the problems associated with this subject of power,[32] except to say that any laws made under it are subject to other provisions of the Constitution. On any view, the States and the Commonwealth could not, therefore, get together to scrap the Constitution as, theoretically, the British Parliament could have done in 1900. There is nothing, however, in the Constitution about the *Colonial Laws Validity Act*, advice to the Queen, or appeals to the Privy Council in respect of State matters. The power, of course, expressly requires the consent of State Parliaments.

The federal Government was anxious to use this power and possibly the external affairs power (which does not require State consent) to effect a constitutional settlement without British enactment. If the power granted initially by the United Kingdom Parliament could (with help from the Statute of Westminster enacted by that Parliament) be used to oust the authority of that Parliament the stream had indeed risen higher than its source. Taken literally, however (and that has been the judicial tendency), section 51 (xxxviii) seemed to provide the necessary power if the external affairs power did not.

As the scope of section 51 (xxxviii) had not been judicially

---

[32] It is discussed in L. Zines (1987) *The High Court and the Constitution*, 2nd edn, Butterworths, Australia, 273–9.

determined, some of the Australian States had doubts. Others considered that the cleanest and most direct way of dealing with this issue was to seek a British enactment. In the upshot there were two *Australia Acts 1986*. One was enacted by the Australian Parliament, following consenting legislation by each State, and one was enacted by the British Parliament at the request and with the consent of the Australian Parliament, in compliance with section 4 of the Statute of Westminster. The Acts are in substantially the same terms and came into operation at exactly the same moment Greenwich Mean Time on 3 March 1986. The long title of each Act is 'An Act to bring constitutional arrangements affecting the Commonwealth and the States into conformity with the status of the Commonwealth of Australia as a sovereign, independent and federal nation'.

In 1989 the High Court took a broad view of section 51 (xxxviii) of the Constitution.[33] That provision was seen as empowering the Commonwealth (with the consent of the relevant States) to make laws with respect to the local exercise of any legislative power which, before federation, could not have been exercised by the legislatures of the former Australian colonies. This construction would, in my view, provide authority for all the provisions of the Australian version of the *Australia Act*, other than the provision in section 15, restricting the manner of repeal or amendment. This latter provision must, I think, rest on British paramount authority because the Constitution does not permit the Commonwealth Parliament to bind its successors.[34]

---

[33] *Port Macdonnell Professional Fishermen's Association Inc v South Australia* (1989) 88 Australian Law Reports 12.
[34] L. Zines (1987) *The High Court and the Constitution*, 2nd edn, Butterworths, Australia, 269–73.

Like the *Canada Act 1982*, the *Australia Act 1986* terminates the power of the Parliament of the United Kingdom to legislate for Australia. Some of its other principal provisions are as follows:

(a) The States can make laws repugnant to Imperial legislation.
(b) The problem of advice to the Queen by the States was resolved by enacting that all the powers and functions of the Queen are exercised *only* by the Governor, except those to appoint and terminate the appointment of the Governor. (However, she is not precluded from exercising her powers when she is personally present in the State.) Advice to the Queen is required to be tendered by the Premier of the State.
(c) Provisions for disallowance and reservation of State legislation are abolished.
(d) Appeals to the Privy Council are abolished.
(e) It is declared that 'Her Majesty's Government in the United Kingdom shall have no responsibility for the government of any State'.
(f) Section 4 of the Statute of Westminster and other anciliary provisions, in their application to Australia, are repealed.
(g) The *Australia Act* and what is left of the Statute of Westminster can be repealed or amended only by the Commonwealth Parliament with the consent of the Parliaments of all the States, subject to any power conferred on the federal Parliament under the amending provision of the Constitution.

So much for Australia. New Zealand entered into its new world of sovereign status with a minimum of fuss, achieving probably the simplest and most uncomplicated constitution in the democratic world. In a practical sense, at any rate, its legislature is the very model of Dicey's notion of a sovereign parliament – even less complicated and elaborate than that of Britain. Having in 1947 decided to adopt the Statute of Westminster, it also secured the enactment by the British Parliament of the *New Zealand Constitution (Amendment) Act 1947*, which conferred on the New Zealand Parliament the power to alter, suspend, or repeal all or any of the provisions of the Constitution granted to New Zealand in 1852. Having achieved a legislature as sovereign as that of the United Kingdom, it then proceeded in 1950 to abolish its upper house, known as the Legislative Council, which had consisted of members nominated for life.

Like Canada, New Zealand recently brought together many of the various instruments that might be said to make up its Constitution and enacted the *Constitution Act 1986*, which came into force on 1 January 1987. As is the case with the *Canada Act* and the *Australia Act*, it declares that no future Act of the United Kingdom Parliament shall henceforth be law in New Zealand. It further declares that the earlier New Zealand Constitution Act and the entire Statute of Westminster 1931 shall cease to have effect.

Strangely enough, the fact that the Australian Constitution has provision for its own amendment has resulted in the federal sphere of government being stuck, for the present, with provisions that do not exist in any of the other countries or in relation to the States of Australia. For example, section 58 of the Constitution empowers the Governor-General to reserve a proposed law for the Queen's assent. Section 59 authorizes the Queen to disallow any law within one year from the Governor-General's assent. I have mentioned that similar State provisions were repealed by the *Australia Act 1986*. Removal of the federal provisions requires a referendum of the people, which is expensive and which Australian Governments are reluctant to initiate.

These provisions were, of course, designed to ensure that Australian legislation did not embarrass the British in the conduct of Imperial and foreign affairs. 'The Queen' meant in political terms the British Government. As a result of the 1926 Conference, the Queen is advised by the Australian Government. The result is that the only practical operation of the disallowance provision would be to enable a Government that could not cause the repeal of an earlier Government's legislation (because of, for example, Senate refusal) simply to have it disallowed by executive action. What was a safeguard for Imperial interests has become a means by which the executive can override Parliament and subvert responsible government. When it was suggested that Mr Whitlam should use this device to get rid of legislation passed in the dying days of the previous Government, he refused on grounds of impropriety. The Constitutional Commission in 1988 recommended the repeal of these provisions.[35]

The Constitution is littered with other outmoded provisions which would, for example, have been removed without question from the *British North America Act* by the British Parliament. Because, however, of the very democratic procedure permitted for altering the Australian Constitution, the federal Government was anxious that it would not be amended in any other way. The bizarre result is that the federal sphere of government in Australia is at present lumbered with colonial relics which do not operate in the States or in the other countries of the Commonwealth.

By a long somewhat complicated process, Canada, Australia, and New Zealand are now constitutionally self-

[35] *Final Report of Constitutional Commission* (1988) para 2.172, Australian Government Publishing Service, Canberra.

sufficient in the sense that any alterations to their frameworks of government can be made, and can only be made, locally. The legislative and executive authorities of the United Kingdom have no more role to play in their affairs.

I suspect, however, that there were many in all three countries and in Britain who were surprised that this result was not achieved until more than half a century after the enactment of the Statute of Westminster, and many years after it was accepted that the countries concerned were internationally sovereign.

The express declarations in the *Canada Act* of 1982, the *Australia Act 1986*, and the *Constitution Act 1986* of New Zealand that no Act of the United Kingdom Parliament shall extend to those countries has resulted in some rethinking of the legal basis for the Constitutions. In Canada this provision clearly owed its force at the time it was made to British legislative power. In Australia there may be dispute as to whether it was made by the federal Parliament in pursuance of its constitutional power or whether the operative Act is the British one.[36] In New Zealand it was accomplished by local law. However, whether in Australia the termination of British legislative power is regarded as an abdication by the Westminster Parliament or as having been achieved by the Australian Parliament with the consent of those of the States, what was done had its ultimate source in power granted in Westminster. The same applies to New Zealand.

There has, therefore, been no attempt to bring about any break in legal continuity or to deny the historical root of constitutional title. Generally speaking, that is a matter about which the people of those countries do not seem to be very fussed, even though they have all been interested in

[36] L. Zines (1987) *The High Court and the Constitution*, 2nd edn, Butterworths, Australia, 269–73.

national symbols in other respects. The affirmation of the Canadian Supreme Court in 1981 of Westminster omnipotence in respect of Canada certainly did not bring an angry nationalist crowd out into the streets. Similarly, there was no public holiday or fireworks on the coming into operation of the *Australia Act* or the *Constitution Act* of New Zealand. It is a reasonable guess that most of the population were unaware of these events.

Even before the passing of this legislation, the traditional view of the legal (as distinct from the historic) source of governmental power in Canada and Australia was questioned. Once section 2 of the Statute of Westminster gave power to override future Imperial Acts, the traditional grundnorm of obedience to the British Parliament began to look very strange. As Brennan J of the High Court of Australia put it, in *Kirmani*:

After the Statute came into effect in a Dominion, it was no longer appropriate to conceive of the future exercise of legislative power by the Parliament of that Dominion as being sustained by a stream of power flowing from a higher Imperial source.[37]

The traditional theories could certainly not sustain the view of Mason, Murphy, and Deane JJ in that case that the operation of Imperial laws in Australia was a matter within the external affairs power because it involved relations with another country. Deane J briefly speculated on the legal theory that would support the Australian constitutional system. He referred to a 'wider foundation which also encompasses the social compact and the international agreement which the Constitution and the Statute [of Westminster] respectively embodied'.[38]

[37] 159 Commonwealth Law Reports 351 at 410.
[38] *Ibid.*, 441–2.

CONSTITUTIONAL AUTONOMY

For Australia, Canada, and New Zealand the starting point of constitutional reasoning now is that the United Kingdom Parliament and Government are not part of the internal legal systems of those countries. Their basic constitutional instruments *were* law because they were enacted by a superior law-maker. They are *now* law because they are accepted as fundamental legal rules of their respective systems and the basic constitutive documents of their communities. The grundnorm of New Zealand society is simply, on this view, the will of its Parliament. (That, however, is a matter I will need to pursue in the next lecture.)

Whether there will be a tendency to elevate 'the People' to a fundamental legal norm is difficult to say. That of course is the position in the United States, and the Canadians have, politically, referred to the patriation of their Constitution in terms of giving power to the people over the Constitution. Australia may have more claim than either to the notion of popular sovereignty, even though the will of the people has not hitherto been referred to as a legal source of power. The Constitution was in fact approved by a majority of the voting electorate in each colony, and the Preamble to the Constitution Act declares that the people of the various colonies agreed to unite in a Commonwealth. The Constitution can be amended, as I have said, only if approved at a referendum.

By contrast, the Constitutions of Canada and New Zealand were the result of requests or demands of representatives and the Constitutions are alterable by the Parliaments. Whether the recognition of a constitutional root of title in the people would make any difference to judicial interpretation of legislative and executive powers in any of these countries is more doubtful. That is a topic which I must return to in the next lecture on entrenchment of individual and democratic rights.

Even if each Constitution is now regarded as the grundnorm without any further legal underpinning, it remains to be seen whether in Canada or Australia this new situation produces any change in constitutional interpretation. In both countries, the courts have, from time to time, insisted that, as the Constitution is an Act of the Imperial Parliament, it must be interpreted as such. Indeed, in 1920, in a landmark decision, the High Court of Australia gave this as one of the reasons for not following United States decisions.[39] The same view was taken by the Privy Council in relation to the Canadian Constitution.[40]

Yet, as all lawyers know, contradictory rules of statutory interpretation hunt in pairs, and rarely resolve ambiguities or uncertainties. In fact, the application of these rules has resulted in very different approaches by judges in Canada and Australia. In other words, I do not believe that the termination of the rule of obedience to the United Kingdom Parliament will, in itself, have any effect on constitutional construction. The attaining of sovereign status has had a very considerable effect in a number of cases, but that had its origins decades ago.

In every sense, therefore, the four countries with which I am concerned here ceased to have common supreme legislature. They retain the same monarch, but that does not mean the same monarchy. At present one single set of laws – the common law and the *Act of Settlement 1700* – govern succession to the throne in all the countries. Any alteration to United Kingdom law on the subject, as occurred in 1936, could not apply to the other three countries. Subject, as

---

[39] *The Engineers Case* (1920) 28 Commonwealth Law Reports 129.
[40] *Attorney-General (Ontario) v Attorney-General (Canada)* [1912] Appeal Cases 571.

always, to a special problem in Australia, it is legally possible therefore that these countries could finish up with different monarchs.

The plenary power of New Zealand would give its Parliament the power to alter the rules of royal succession. I would have thought also that federal residual power in Canada would clearly authorize such rules. A highly respected Canadian authority has suggested, however, that to change the rules of royal succession for Canada would amount to a constitutional amendment which would require the unanimous consent of the Canadian Provinces.[41] This view is probably based on section 38 of the Constitution Act 1982 which provides for the amendment to the Canadian Constitution in relation to, among other things, 'the office of the Queen'. The Canadian Constitution, however, does not contain rules for succession to the throne. Those rules seem to apply in Canada by virtue of the common law and the *Act of Settlement*.

There is no express power in the Australian Parliament on this subject. The Advisory Committee to the Constitutional Commission on Executive Government, chaired by Sir Zelman Cowen, refrained, in its report in 1987, from making any recommendations for power to be expressly conferred on federal Parliament to make laws relating to royal succession. It declared that it was unlikely that Australia would retain the monarchy if it resulted in a different monarch from that in the United Kingdom.[42]

Yet, as I mentioned, this could come about by the British rather than the Australians changing the rules. Power

[41] P. W. Hogg (1985) *Constitutional Law of Canada*, 2nd edn, Carswell, Toronto, 33 n. 8.
[42] *Report of Advisory Committee on Executive Government* (1987) 7–8, Australian Government Publishing Service, Canberra.

therefore might be needed to ensure that Australia *has* the same monarch as the United Kingdom.

Some have maintained that the Australian Constitution requires that the sovereign shall be the same as that in the United Kingdom. The argument is based on section 2 of the *Commonwealth of Australia Constitution Act*, which provides:

The provisions of this Act referring to the Queen shall extend to Her Majesty's heirs and successors in the sovereignty of the United Kingdom.

The argument is that this provision, rather than the *Act of Settlement*, provides the rule of royal succession in Australia. In other words, it requires that the monarch of Australia should always be the monarch of the United Kingdom. The view taken by the Constitutional Commission, however, was that put forward by Sir Kenneth Bailey fifty years ago. He said that the provision does not supplant the *Act of Settlement* as the succession law of Australia, but merely makes it clear that references to the Queen include her successors according to law from time to time.[43] This view is supported by the fact that a similar provision in the *British North America Act* was omitted by the *Statute Law Revision Act 1893* of the United Kingdom, following the enactment of the *Interpretation Act 1889*, which provided that references to the Queen included her successors.

As I have said, the Australian Parliament has no express power to make laws relating to succession to the throne. It is likely that the High Court would hold that there was a power inherent in nationhood, particularly as otherwise

[43] K. Bailey, 'The Abdication Legislation in the United Kingdom and in the Dominions' (1938) 3 *Politica* 1 at 17–18: *Final Report of Constitutional Commission* (1988) para 2.157–2.161, Australian Government Publishing Service, Canberra.

there would be no other parliament that could deal with the subject. It is clearly not a matter of State power. Another possibility is the use of the power in section 51 (xxxviii), referred to earlier in relation to the *Australia Act*. The Constitutional Commission recommended that there be an express power with respect to 'succession to the throne and regency in the sovereignty of Australia'.[44]

Even while these countries have the same monarch, it is clear that the former one and indivisible Crown is now disintegrated into its various national components. The monarch in the four countries is in a position similar to that which occurred in relation to England and Scotland between 1603 and 1707 or during the Hanoverian period.

In 1982 the British Court of Appeal declared that in matters of law and government the Queen of the United Kingdom is entirely independent and distinct from the Queen of Canada.[45] On 13 September 1988 the High Court of Australia held an English-born British subject, who had gone to Australia at the age of nine in 1957, to be an 'alien' for the purposes of federal power to make laws with respect to 'aliens'. There is no doubt that such a person would not have been regarded as within the aliens power when the Constitution was enacted in 1900.[46] A few years earlier Gibbs CJ declared that 'the allegiance that Australians owe to Her Majesty is owed not as British subjects, but as subjects of the Queen of Australia'.[47] It seems to be accepted that the

---

[44] *Final Report of Constitutional Commission* (1988) para 2.166, Australian Government Publishing Service, Canberra.
[45] *Re. Secretary of State for Foreign and Commonwealth Affairs; Ex parte Indian Association of Alberta* [1982] Queens Bench 892.
[46] *Nolan v Minister for Immigration and Ethnic Affairs* (1988) 80 Australian Law Reports 561.
[47] *Pochi v Macphee* (1981) 151 Commonwealth Law Reports 101, 109.

several references in the Australian Constitution to 'a subject of the Queen' now mean a subject of the Queen in the right of Australia.[48]

Thus the institutions of an Imperial Crown and an Imperial Parliament have come to an end. It is remarkable, however, that it has taken sixty years after the Balfour Declaration to finally achieve that result in the remaining 'old Dominions' of the Commonwealth.

[48] *Street v Queensland Bar Association* (1989) 88 Australian Law Reports 321.

2

THE ENTRENCHMENT OF INDIVIDUAL AND DEMOCRATIC RIGHTS

Nineteenth-century and early twentieth-century complacency regarding individual rights in Britain, and a certain contempt for countries that had a need for entrenched constitutional rights, were reflected in the 'old Dominions'. The common law, British justice, and remedies such as habeas corpus and the prerogative writs, were regarded as of more worth in protecting the individual than elaborate and exotic lists of abstract rights in foreign countries.

While certain rights of this nature appeared in the Australian Constitution, they certainly didn't amount to a fully fledged Bill of Rights, and in any case most of them were binding only on the federal as distinct from the State Governments.[1] Perhaps the general attitude in all these countries could be summed up in the remark made by a former Australian Chief Justice, Sir Harry Gibbs, that 'If society is tolerant and rational, it does not need a Bill of Rights. If it is not, no Bill of Rights will preserve it.'[2]

---

[1] They include freedom of religion (s 116), just terms for the acquisition of property (s 51 (xxxi)) and trial by jury for indictable offences (s 80).

[2] Quoted in *Final Report of the Constitutional Commission* (1988) para 9.101, Australian Government Publishing Service, Canberra.

Faith in majoritarian democracy was firmly established in all four countries by the early twentieth century. This reinforced the legal principle of the supremacy of Parliament. The obedience paid by the courts to what was sometimes called 'the will of Parliament' was politically justified on the basis of democratic principle, reflecting Dicey's distinction between the 'legal sovereign' (Parliament) and the 'political sovereign' (the electorate).

But if democracy was the prime concept justifying this basic legal principle, it was argued that at least democratic structures needed constitutional protection. While all four countries eventually had a system of adult suffrage and secret ballot, that did not prevent gross disproportion between electoral preference and the number of seats in Parliament, or Governments which were supported by only a minority of the people. The uneven value of each voter's vote, the gerrymandering of electorates and constituencies, the difficulty of minority parties gaining seats in Parliament, and the power of interest groups and the bureaucracy made the democratic theory of the supremacy of Parliament seem at times rather tatty. Assuming that the main argument against judicial review of legislation is that the democratic determination of policy issues was preferable to that of unelected and technically irresponsible judges, it was said that a Constitution should at least safeguard the democratic process.[3]

The very notion of a free election, however, assumes certain liberties, such as freedom of expression, of assembly, and of association. Thus, provisions concerned with the establishment and maintenance of democratic processes

---

[3] For example, H. W. R. Wade (1980) *Constitutional Fundamentals*, chapter 2, Stevens, London.

appear, to some degree, to shade into those which are thought desirable by people who emphasize, not merely democratic structures, but the liberty of the individual and the protection of minorities.

But, of course, the attack on the principle of the sovereignty of Parliament went much further. The political decline of Parliament and the ascendancy of the Executive, and of the Prime Minister in particular, over the Parliament has been a familiar theme for many decades. The rise of centralized tightly controlled political parties, the power of the bureaucracy, the power of the Prime Minister to call an election at any time, and the near powerless state of the Opposition have all been the subject of a vast literature and need no repeating.

There has also been concern shown that all these factors have resulted in a feeling of hopelessness and alienation by various persons and groups from the political system, because of the inability to have their voices heard and their arguments considered and debated on particular issues. This has led in some of these countries (and particularly in Australia) to calls for the introduction of the initiative and referendum whereby a substantial minority may ensure that its views on individual measures may receive democratic consideration.[4]

In the present state of affairs, however, the only obvious constitutional check on overweening executive power seems to me to be the judiciary. In all the countries with which I am concerned, the judiciary is held in high social regard. On the other hand, one of the arguments of those opposed to a Bill of Rights has been that, if adopted, it would

[4] For example, G. Walker (1987) *Initiative and referendum: the people's law*, Centre for Independent Studies, St Leonards, NSW.

threaten and perhaps destroy the highly important position the courts occupy in our communities – a view which has not been borne out in the United States or in European countries.

The concept of the courts as the guardians of our liberties is an old one, even if the behaviour of the judges over the centuries has been rather erratic in this regard. Judges are of course creatures of their time (or the time before). Matters regarded as of social or moral importance will vary from generation to generation. This will be reflected eventually in the swings of the judicial pendulum.

When I was a student, in Sydney, in the early 1950s, Sir Raymond Evershed, Master of the Rolls (as he then was), explained to us that it was believed by many when the Attlee Government was elected in 1945 that, based on past performance, the courts of England would emasculate any social welfare or other collectivist legislation of that Government. Imbued with notions of individualism, freedom of contract, property rights, and the adversary process, the judges would, it was said, be either unable or unwilling to interpret and apply the legislation according to its spirit and intendment. The Master of the Rolls then remarked that he was pleased to say that that had not happened. The judges had not sabotaged the social welfare state.

About a decade or so later, however, the wind was blowing from the opposite direction. There was much legislation conferring broad discretions and fact-finding functions on a vast array of ministers, officials, and tribunals. Provisions were inserted expressly to prevent the courts from intervening in the administrative process or from reviewing decisions. Decisions directly affecting rights, duties, and expectations were made behind closed doors, with no reasons given. Many a citizen, it was remarked, felt rather like the hero or, rather, victim in Kafka's *The Trial*.

From the mid-1960s the courts took up the challenge. Professor Sir William Wade has in several works detailed the extraordinary development over the past quarter-century of judicial control of administrative and executive action in Britain,[5] which was reflected in Canada, Australia, and New Zealand. (Indeed, the process has been taken further in the federal sphere in Australia by legislation. For example, the simple statutory requirement of requiring reasons to be given for decisions has immeasurably enhanced the power of the courts to control the administration.)[6] So far has this trend gone that some administrative lawyers, who had welcomed the new approach to administrative law, have expressed fear that there is a danger that the judges will take out of the hands of officials and tribunals matters that should be within their jurisdiction. Some have reverted to the fears and expectations of which Lord Evershed spoke all those years ago.[7] However, none of this touched the basic principle of the non-reviewability of Acts of Parliament.

Before all this began, Britain became a party to the European Convention of Human Rights in 1951. In 1966 it accepted the provision allowing individuals to refer matters to the European Human Rights Commission and accepted the jurisdiction of the European Court on Human Rights. It has regularly renewed at five-yearly intervals its acknow-

[5] W. H. R. Wade (1982) *Administrative Law*, 5th edn, Clarendon, Oxford.
[6] *Administrative Decisions (Judicial Review Act) 1977*.
[7] For example, J. A. G. Griffith (1985) *The Politics of the Judiciary* (3rd edn) Fontana, London; Dennis Pearce, 'Judicial Review of Tribunal Decisions – The Need for Restraint' (1981) 12 Federal Law Review 167.

ledgement of the right of individual petition. The result of these acts of the British Government has been, from the viewpoint of the outside observer, extraordinary.

The United Kingdom has been a frequent defendant before both bodies. In many cases its statutory law and its common law have been found deficient, that is to say as not measuring up to the standards of the Convention. Cases against the United Kingdom which have resulted in adverse findings of the European Court on Human Rights have included complaints about restrictions on the correspondence of prisoners,[8] the treatment in Northern Ireland of suspected terrorists,[9] birching by judicial order,[10] criminal laws relating to homosexual conduct,[11] the inadequacies of the writ of habeas corpus to review the confinement of a patient in a mental hospital,[12] telephone tapping by the police,[13] and the effect of the law relating to contempt of court on freedom of the press.[14] Many of these decisions have caused the Government to procure changes in legislation or in practices to achieve conformity with the pronouncements of the European Court. There may be some tendency (although it is not entirely clear) for British judges

---

[8] *Golder v United Kingdom* (1975) 1 European Human Rights Reports 524; *Silver v United Kingdom* (1983) 5 European Human Rights Reports 347.

[9] *Republic of Ireland v United Kingdom* (1978) 2 European Human Rights Reports 25.

[10] *Tyrer v United Kingdom* (1978) 2 European Human Rights Reports 1.

[11] *Dudgeon v United Kingdom* (1981) 4 European Human Rights Reports 149. See also (1983) 5 European Human Rights Reports 573.

[12] *X v United Kingdom* (1981) 5 European Human Rights Reports 192. See also (1982) 4 European Human Rights Reports 118.

[13] *Malone v United Kingdom* (1984) 7 European Human Rights Reports 14.

[14] *The Sunday Times v United Kingdom* (1979) 2 European Human Rights Reports 245. See also (1980) 3 European Human Rights Reports 317.

to have regard to the Convention and the decisions of the European Court in developing or changing common law rules.[15]

Because of many of the factors I have mentioned and, to some degree, the activity of the European Court of Human Rights, a movement developed from the early 1960s to provide Britain with something in the nature of a judicially enforceable Bill of Rights. About twenty bills in the same number of years were introduced into Parliament. Several passed the House of Lords and came to grief in the Commons. In recent times, the tendency, in such Bills, has been to attempt to incorporate into domestic law the provisions of the European Convention.[16]

Apart from some judicial pronouncements north of the border, chiefly relating to the Act of Union,[17] there has been no challenge by the courts to the supremacy of Parliament in Britain; but some judges in the other three countries, from time to time, became restless with the doctrine. A written constitution, of course, provides more scope for judges to construe provisions according to notions of civil liberty and the rule of law, even where the Constitution does not contain any express provisions protecting individual or democratic rights.

Sometimes the interpretation of legislative powers in a

---

[15] *Raymond v Honey* [1983] 1 Appeal Cases 1; *Attorney-General v BBC* [1981] Appeal Cases 303, 352, 354, 362; *Garland v British Rail Engineering Ltd* [1983] 2 Appeal Cases 751; *Malone v Metropolitan Police Commissioner* [1979] Chancery Division 344.

[16] This was also recommended by the Northern Ireland Standing Advisory Committee on Human Rights, Command Paper 7009 (1977) and by a majority of the House of Lords Select Committee on a Bill of Rights, House of Lords Paper 176, June 1978.

[17] *MacCormick v Lord Advocate* [1953] Session Cases 396.

federation may achieve libertarian ends.[18] In Australia, the High Court held invalid the *Communist Party Dissolution Act* 1950 which purported, *inter alia*, to dissolve that party and any other organizations that had a significant communist membership if the Governor-General in Council was 'satisfied' (among other things) that the continued existence of the body would be prejudicial to the security and defence of the Commonwealth or to the execution or maintenance of the Constitution or laws of the Commonwealth. The Act was held not to be within the authority of the Parliament to make laws with respect to defence or the preservation of the Constitution. This was because the Act made the constitutional question, that is the relevance of the body to the defence of the Commonwealth or the preservation of the Constitution, dependent purely on legislative judgement in the case of the Australian Communist Party, itself, and on executive judgement in the case of other bodies. This had been permitted in a time of total war, but was held not to be supported by the international circumstances that existed in 1950. A major reason for rejecting the Government's arguments was stated by Sir Owen Dixon as follows:

The Constitution ... is an instrument framed in accordance with many traditional conceptions ... Among these I think that it may fairly be said that the rule of law forms an assumption.[19]

In determining the extent of federal power to organize the celebration of the bicentennial of European settlement in Australia, it was held that Commonwealth law could not

[18] *Australian Communist Party v Commonwealth* (1951) 83 Commonwealth Law Reports 1; *Adelaide Company of Jehovah's Witnesses Inc v Commonwealth* (1943) 67 Commonwealth Law Reports 116; *Switzman v Elbling* [1957] Supreme Court Reports 285.
[19] (1951) 83 Commonwealth Law Reports 1, 193.

validly prevent the use of certain words and symbols by persons other than the corporation that the Commonwealth had created to organize the celebrations. Brennan J declared that 'freedom of speech can hardly be an incidental casualty of an activity undertaken by the Executive Government to advance a nation which boasts of its freedom'.[20] In that case some Aborigines used the words and symbols to oppose and attack the celebrations.[21]

Having regard to civil liberty in determining a distribution of powers in a federation does not of course establish a bill of rights, because if the matter does not come within the federal power it will usually belong to the States or Provinces and vice versa, but the threat may come from only one quarter in the particular circumstances. Thus, in Canada in *Switzman v Elbling*[22] the Supreme Court held invalid a law of Quebec prohibiting the use of a house to propagate communism. The law was labelled 'criminal law' (a federal subject) and not 'property' (a Provincial subject). Some judges followed an earlier case, *Re Alberta Statutes*[23] where there was direct resort by Duff CJ and Cannon J to freedom of speech as being of such importance that it could be regarded only as a national value and not a civil right 'in the Province'. It seems that in these cases similar laws emanating from the Canadian Parliament were unlikely.[24] In relation to the communist legislation in Australia there was the reverse situation.

Other principles relevant to civil liberty may be inferred

---

[20] *Davis v Commonwealth* (1988) 82 Australian Law Reports 633, 657.
[21] See also Mason CJ, Deane and Gaudron, JJ at 645.
[22] [1957] Supreme Court Reports 286.
[23] [1938] Supreme Court Reports 100.
[24] Weiler, 'The Supreme Court and the Law of Canadian Federalism' (1973) 23, *University of Toronto Law Journal* 307, 342–52.

from the structure of, or basic concepts in, the Constitution. For example, the reference to 'an election' in the Canadian and Australian Constitutions might provide an opportunity for courts to imply a degree of freedom of speech and association. In the case of the Constitutions of Australia and Ceylon the courts implied a separation of the judicial power that is not clearly expressed in those Constitutions.

Sometimes the protection of the individual arises in unlikely contexts. For example, section 109 of the Australian Constitution provides that when a law of a State is inconsistent with a law of the Commonwealth the latter shall prevail, and the former shall, to the extent of the inconsistency, be invalid. In 1983 the High Court had held that a State law was invalid on this ground, because federal law had 'covered the field'. The federal Parliament attempted to amend the legislation retrospectively so as to give the State law a valid operation from the time of its enactment. Generally speaking, the heads of federal power in the Constitution authorize the making of retrospective laws. The Court held, however, that the amendment could not retrospectively revive the State law. One of the reasons was that s109 had to be interpreted as a protection of the individual and not merely as a provision concerned with the distribution of legislative powers. It was, the majority judges thought, important that the individual know at any time which law to obey. Deane J declared that 'the provisions of the Constitution should be properly viewed as ultimately concerned with the governance and protection of the people from whom the artificial entities called Commonwealth and States derive their authority'.[25]

[25] *University of Wollongong v Metwally* (1984) 56 Australian Law Reports 1, 21.

These devices and implications from particular provisions of the Constitution are however no substitute for specific Bills of Rights provisions, and do not satisfy those who want broad restrictions on the power of government based on principles inherent in a liberal and democratic state. In Canada, Australia, and New Zealand, in recent times, some judges have not accepted as calmly as British judges the principle that any legislative act (otherwise within power) is law no matter how evil or horrendous its provisions.

The pegs on which to hang reasons for finding inherent or assumed limits on legislative power have varied in the three countries. In all of them, they are (or in the case of Canada were) no more than straws in the wind; but the very fact that judges have pronounced upon them or have indicated the possibility of such restrictions has startled some and shocked others.

Apart from the Canadian Bill of Rights and the Charter of Rights and Freedoms (which I will discuss later), some Canadian judges found implied in the *British North America Act* what was in effect a Bill of Rights. In cases, referred to above, invalidating Provincial laws to require newspapers to give the Government a right of reply to criticism and to prevent the use of a house for the purpose of propagating communism,[26] some judges left open the possibility that such laws were denied to all Canadian legislatures, and that the *British North America Act* (now the *Constitution Act*) contained an implied Bill of Rights. Two devices were relied on. One was the statement in the Preamble to the Act of 1867 which refers to 'a Constitution similar in principle to that of the United Kingdom'. This line of reasoning is no doubt

---

[26] *Re. Alberta Press Statutes* [1936] Supreme Court Reports 100; *Switzman v Elbling* [1957] Supreme Court Reports 285.

strange to those British constitutional lawyers who have in recent years urged the entrenchment in Britain of individual rights and other restrictions on parliamentary power. The reasoning is that the intention of the Act was that Canadians were to enjoy whatever liberties existed in the United Kingdom in 1867. As has been pointed out, the argument is weak and is easily met by the proposition that the sovereignty of Parliament was the central feature of the United Kingdom Constitution at that date.

The other argument based on the constitutional creation of representative governmental institutions is similar to one that I have mentioned. It would, however, limit the rights to those that might broadly be described as political or democratic.[27] Four years before the enactment of the Charter a majority of the Supreme Court appeared to express the view that there were no fundamental rights that were outside legislative power to control.[28] In more recent times, however, there has been a revival of the notion of implied rights, apart from the Charter of Rights and Freedom. In *SDGMR v Dolphin Delivery Ltd*[29] McIntyre J (speaking for the Court) referred to the views expressed in earlier cases regarding freedom of speech as an essential feature of Canadian parliamentary democracy and added 'Indeed this Court may be said to have given it constitutional status'. This passage was quoted with approval by Dickson CJ in *OPSEU v Attorney-General for Ontario*.[30] Also, in that case, Beetz J, speaking for four judges of the Court, declared that 'the

[27] P. W. Hogg (1985) *Canadian Constitutional Law*, 2nd edn, Carswell, Toronto, 635–8.
[28] *Attorney-General (Canada) and Dupond v Montreal* [1978] 2 Supreme Court Reports 770, 796.
[29] [1986] 2 Supreme Court Reports 573 at 584.
[30] [1987] 2 Supreme Court Reports 2 at 25.

essential structure of free Parliamentary institutions' could not, apart from Charter considerations, be impaired by federal or provincial legislation.[31]

In Australia the boldest attempt to infer in the Constitution a fully fledged Bill of Rights binding on all Governments was made by Murphy J. He stated that the Constitution assumed a 'free and democratic society' and read into the Constitution a large number of varied restrictions on the powers of both the Commonwealth and the States. From this starting point of a free and democratic society, he found that there was to be inferred, subject to necessary social exceptions, the prohibition of slavery and serfdom and freedom of movement and communication.[32] He further considered that the legislative powers of the Australian Parliaments did not extend to authorizing sexual discrimination[33] or cruel or unusual punishments.[34]

Generally, His Honour did not relate these suggested limitations to any specific provisions of the Constitution. In one case, however, in explaining why the federal Parliament could not provide for cruel or unusual punishments, he seized on the phrase 'peace, order and good government of the Commonwealth' which qualifies all the express powers granted to the federal Parliament.[35] I shall have to refer to this phrase again later. For the present it is enough to say that it had always been considered as indicating broad plenary power. It had earlier been held that the only

[31] *Ibid.* at 57.
[32] *McGraw-Hinds (Aust) Pty Ltd v Smith* (1979) 144 Commonwealth Law Reports 633, 667–70; *Buck v Bavone* (1976) 135 Commonwealth Law Reports 110.
[33] *Ansett Transport Industries (Operations) Pty Ltd v Wardley* (1980) 142 Commonwealth Law Reports 237.
[34] *Sillery v The Queen* (1981) 35 Australian Law Reports 227.
[35] *Ibid.*, 237.

restriction on power to be derived from this wording was a territorial one.[36]

Murphy J's attempt to put a full-scale Bill of Rights into the Constitution by a process of implication was not taken up by other High Court judges, but, as was the case in Canada, some judges have made tantalizing suggestions from time to time that the nature of the polity might make certain types of laws invalid. In one recent case, for example, Deane J suggested that there may be 'an implication of the underlying equality of the people of the Commonwealth under the law of the Constitution'.[37] If this view were followed, Australia might, by judicial creation, have an implied provision guaranteeing equal protection of the laws similar to that in the United States Constitution, even though (I might add) the framers expressly decided against such a clause.

In respect of Canada and the Federal Government of Australia there are of course rigid Constitutions which are subject to judicial interpretation and exegesis. That is not the case in Britain or New Zealand nor (subject to the federal Constitution) is it, generally speaking, the position of the Australian States. In all these cases there seemed scant opportunities for discovery of rights or liberties in the nooks or crannies of the Constitution. The supremacy of Parliament has been assumed for ages to be the governing principle. In the last few years, however, there have been judges of New Zealand and of New South Wales who have suggested what had hitherto been regarded as unthinkable,

---

[36] The principles are discussed in *Union Steamship Co of Australia Pty Ltd v King* (1988) 82 Australian Law Reports 43.
[37] *Queensland Electricity Commission v Commonwealth* (1985) 159 Commonwealth Law Reports 192 at 247–8.

namely that some Acts of Parliament might be invalid because of their repressive nature.

Among the four countries I have been discussing, New Zealand stands out as having the simplest constitutional framework – no federal system, no entrenched restrictions on power,[38] no Upper House, and a system of responsible government that generally ensures ultimate control by the Executive of the Legislature. There is, therefore, nothing in the way of constitutional checks and balances, even to the extent that exists in the United Kingdom in the form of the power of the House of Lords to delay legislation. Indeed, so familiar were Governments at ruling the roost, unhindered by anything but political considerations, that on one occasion, in 1976, the Government directed the public service not to administer the law because it intended to obtain its amendment or repeal at the next session of Parliament. The court compared the Prime Minister with James II in exercising a supposed dispensing power.[39]

Into this executive paradise the President of the Court of Appeal of New Zealand has intruded comments which, if adopted by the courts, would detract considerably from Parliament's supposed omnipotence. In a series of cases Sir Robin Cooke declared that there were some common law rights that may go so deep that even Parliament could not destroy them. He instanced the liberty of the citizen to resort to the ordinary courts for the determination of their

---

[38] Section 189 of the *Electoral Act* 1956 purports to prevent any amendment of the central provisions of that Act unless 75 per cent of the Parliament agree or a referendum approves. It seems that this provision can be repealed by the ordinary process.

[39] *Fitzgerald v Muldoon* [1976] 2 New Zealand Law Reports 615.

rights and the right of the citizen not to be compelled, by torture for example, to make a confession.[40]

The judgements concerned do not provide any reasoning or analysis in relation to this conclusion. They are, however, clearly in the spirit of Sir Edward Coke's famous pronouncement in *Dr Bonham's Case*[41] and are absolutely opposed to Dicey.

The Parliaments of the States of Australia are, of course, far more restricted in their legislative power than is the New Zealand Parliament. Some powers were taken away from them by the Australian Constitution and their laws, otherwise within power, are liable to be rendered inoperative by valid inconsistent federal laws. Nevertheless, this leaves a large area within which they may make laws. The usual formula in provisions conferring legislative power in State constitutional instruments is that the Parliament may make laws 'for the peace, order and good government' of the State. In New South Wales the phrase is 'for the peace, welfare and good government'. Section 2(2) of the *Australia Act 1986* declares that the legislative powers of each State include all powers 'that the Parliament of the United Kingdom might have exercised ... for the peace, order and good government of that State'.

In 1986, a New South Wales law purported to confer executive power to deregister a named State trade union. Deregistration deprives the union of status under the industrial arbitration laws. A challenge to the deregistration was dismissed by a single judge of the Supreme Court of New

---

[40] *Fraser v State Services Commission* [1984] 1 New Zealand Law Reports 116, 121; *Taylor v New Zealand Poultry Board* [1984] 1 New Zealand Law Reports 394, 398; *New Zealand Drivers' Association v New Zealand Road Carriers* [1982] 1 New Zealand Law Reports 374, 390.

[41] (1610) 8 Coke's Reports 114.

South Wales. The union appealed to the Court of Appeal of that State. Before the appeal was heard, Parliament enacted another law 'to remove doubts'. Among other things, it validated the ministerial action taken. The validity of the latter Act was challenged in the Court of Appeal, but the action was dismissed.

One ground for challenge was that the Act interfered with the judicial process and was invalid. The Court held, in accordance with precedent, that that was irrelevant, as the separation of powers doctrine did not apply within the State sphere. The trade union then, in a spirit, no doubt, of desperation, argued that the Act was bad because, being *ad hominem* legislation, it was inconsistent with fundamental rights, including the right to natural justice. There is little doubt that, say, twenty years ago any counsel daring to make such a submission would have got short shrift from the court. On this occasion, however, a full court of five was convened to hear it. The judgements ranged widely over the fundamental rules and principles of British-style constitutional law. The union did not succeed, but the case gave an opportunity to some judges, including the Chief Justice of the State, to indicate that, in their view, Dicey's principle did not apply to the Parliament of New South Wales.

Street CJ declared that the words 'peace, welfare and good government of New South Wales' were a substantial limitation on legislative power. 'New South Wales' referred not to the territory or people, but 'the body politic' as 'a Parliamentary democracy' – 'an entity ruled by a democratically elected Parliament whose citizens enjoy the great inherited privileges of freedom and justice under the protection of an independent judiciary'. It was, therefore, for the court to determine whether a law satisfied the description of being for the 'peace', the 'welfare', and the 'good government' of that polity. If it did not, it would be struck down as unconstitutional. Two examples he gave of State laws that would be unconstitutional were laws taking away universal suffrage or interfering with the independence of the judiciary.

Dr Bonham's Case was partly resurrected: 'This brave assertion has not stood the test of time . . . But the ringing words of Lord Coke . . . may yet provide encouragement for courts in putting down tyrannous legislation.' While His Honour was also very taken with the dicta of Sir Robin Cooke in New Zealand, he felt unable to follow them, preferring to look to the phrase 'peace, welfare and good government' as the source of power in the courts to protect 'our Parliamentary democracy'. Priestley J considered the position arguable and thought that, whatever the position in Britain, it might be that the New South Wales courts could strike down Leslie Stephen's hypothetical statute requiring that all blue-eyed babies be put to death.[42]

If these principles were to obtain acceptance by the High Court of Australia, they would operate in relation to the federal power also. As I mentioned earlier, Murphy J on at least one occasion rested his implied Bill of Rights on a similar phrase in the Commonwealth Constitution.

The extraordinary upsurge in judicial boldness in challenging legislatures in the cause of individual and democratic liberties and the rule of law, in Canada, Australia, and New Zealand, corresponds with the vastly increased checks that British judges, and those of the other countries, have

---

[42] *Building Construction Employees and Builders' Labourers Federation of NSW v Minister for Industrial Relations* (1986) 7 New South Wales Law Reports 372. Glass, J. A. (at 407) reserved his position. It was rejected by Kirby P (at 404) and Mahoney JA (at 413).

imposed upon executive and administrative authority over the last twenty years or so, but it is, of course, more radical.

Because of the Charter of Rights, it is not a major issue any more in Canada. In 1988 the High Court of Australia declared that the words 'peace, order and good government' do not confer on the courts jurisdiction to strike down legislation on the ground that, in the opinion of a court, it does not promote or secure the peace, order, or good government of the State. They left open the question whether the exercise of legislative power was, as Cooke P had suggested, subject to some restraint by reference to 'rights deeply rooted in our democratic system of government and the common law'.[43] I do not think that in the long run the High Court of Australia is likely to approve an implied full Bill of Rights in Australia. I am less sure of New Zealand. There are of course no signs of it in Britain. What is significant, however, is the number of otherwise respectable, and in some cases respected, judges prepared to challenge an accepted legal dogma that goes back two centuries or more and on which all lawyers in British countries were weaned.

If this trend should develop further, it seems to me that it would be highly dangerous and certainly undesirable. This is not because I am of the view that there should be no limitations on parliamentary power. It is simply that these efforts to create legislative restrictions, which are not based on any specific provisions, provide no guidance or check to judicial aggrandisement or personal predilections. I agree with Kirby P, President of the New South Wales Court of Appeal, that these notions should be rejected 'because, once allowed, there is no logical limit to their ambit'.[44]

[43] *Union Steamship Co. of Australia Pty Ltd v King* (1988) 82 Australian Law Reports 43.
[44] (1986) 7 New South Wales Law Reports 374 at 405.

It is not necessary, therefore, to approve of, say, Professor J. Griffith's view to support this thesis, nor do I ignore the fact that the judicial function in interpreting any Bill or Charter of Rights must confer large discretionary and policy-making power on judges. I am not totally distrustful of judges when it comes to the protection of the individual or of minorities. But I suggest that they should not be given, nor should they grab, a blank cheque.

The drafting of Acts, constitutional provisions, or treaties relating to rights and freedoms needs very careful consideration. Those in existence differ in their provisions, even when confined to the negative freedoms of a liberal society. They should provide at least guidelines for the judges who have to interpret them. Accepting that entrenched rights confer on the judiciary broad policy-making powers it is necessary to give deliberate attention to the extent and limits of this judicial power. To accept only 'peace, welfare and good government' (as Street CJ does) or 'a free and democratic society' (as Murphy J did) or 'deeply held common law principles' (as Cooke P does) as the starting point in reasoning is to invite a judge to discover in the Constitution his or her own broad political philosophy.

Generally, existing and proposed rights in these four countries have shied away from entrenching economic policy, whether related to social welfare, employment, or economic liberalism. For many years faith in judges in dealing with social and economic policy issues was shaken by the experience of the United States Supreme Court between, say, 1900 and 1936 when it imposed a *laissez faire* philosophy on the country. It achieved this mainly by the interpretation of the clause in the Fifth and Fourteenth Amendments preventing the federal and State Governments and Legislatures from depriving any person of life, liberty, or property without due process of law.[45]

The classic case was *Lochner v New York*,[46] which declared invalid a State law providing for a maximum working day of ten hours and a maximum working week of sixty hours for bakery workers. The main ground of invalidity was that the Act interfered with the freedom of an employer or employee to enter into contracts freely. This freedom was, the court held, guaranteed by the Fourteenth Amendment and could be restricted only on grounds of public safety, health, morality, or welfare. In the court's view the interest of the public was 'not in the slightest degree affected' by the Act under consideration. It amounted to 'mere meddlesome interference with the rights of the individual'. Holmes J, in dissent, said that the majority had decided the case upon an economic theory that a large part of the country did not support. Other provisions held invalid upon similar grounds included those providing for minimum wages for women and children and a federal law making it an offence for a railroad company to discharge a worker on the grounds of membership of a trade union.[47]

All this was no doubt in the recent memory of those Ministers in the Attlee Government, such as Jowett and Cripps, who (Anthony Lester has pointed out) were fearful of the draft European Convention on Human Rights, claiming that it was inconsistent with the planned economy which they were in the process of erecting.[48] While I believe they

[45] *Lochner v New York* (1905) 198 United States Reports 45.
[46] (1905) 198 United States Reports 45.
[47] *Adair v US* (1908) 208 United States Reports 161; *Adkins v Children's Hospital* (1923) 261 United States Reports 525.
[48] Lester, 'Fundamental Rights: The United Kingdom Isolated?' [1984] *Public Law* 46.

were wrong, the American experience in the early twentieth century and the anxiety of the Labour ministers in the 1940s does underline an important point. In three of the four countries I am considering – the United Kingdom, Australia, and New Zealand – economic individualism and collectivism have, to a degree, been the features which have distinguished the major political parties. Constitutional entrenchment of, say, freedom of contract, enterprise, or the free use and disposal of property could favour one side of the political battle. If all this could be achieved by construction of the words 'liberty' and 'property' and 'due process of law', how much more dangerous for judges to be in a position to entrench rights based only on what they would regard as required by a free society, or as consistent with peace, order, and good government.

In the case of New Zealand (and of course Britain) there would be a further factor. This is no written Constitution, and, if the unwritten judicially created Constitution restricts Parliament, who can override the judges? There would presumably be no amending procedure. Parliament could not give itself power which the judge-made Constitution denied to it. In New South Wales, if Parliament attempted to delete the words 'peace, welfare and good government' from the *Constitution Act*, the issue would arise whether this would be invalid because it was inconsistent with the peace, welfare, and good government of New South Wales.

This does not lead inevitably to supporting the doctrine of parliamentary sovereignty or to ignoring the dangers of 'elected tyranny'. In all four countries, the debate about some formal entrenchment of individual and democratic rights has continued. It has, up to now, come to fruition only in Canada. In a sense, however, the European Convention provides a practical check on parliamentary power (as unsatisfactory as it is) in Britain that is absent from the other two countries. Indeed the Chief Justice of Australia has recently said (referring to entrenched rights) that 'Australia and New Zealand are virtually alone in standing outside the mainstream of legal development'. He added that the content of British law will be steadily influenced by the European Convention and by EEC law and that 'this will affect the traditional affinity between Australian law and English law and serve to emphasize our legal isolation'.[49]

As a result of the *Constitution Act 1982* Canada has an entrenched Charter of Rights and Freedoms. The form of the Charter was influenced greatly by the International Convention on Civil and Political Rights and by the European Convention for the Protection of Human Rights and Fundamental Freedoms. It is binding in respect of any executive or legislative functions in the central or Provincial spheres of government. The provisions are in three broad categories, leaving aside provisions relating to language and educational rights and the Canadian Indians. They are:

(a) Democratic provisions, including the right to vote, periodic elections, and annual meetings of Parliament.
(b) Individual freedoms, including religion, conscience, thought, belief, expression, peaceful assembly, association, and movement.
(c) Minimum standards of the criminal justice system, including the prohibition of unusual punishments, unreasonable search and seizures, and retrospective offences. There are also various rights for those arrested or detained, including that of the presumption of innocence.

[49] A. Mason, 'A Bill of Rights for Australia': Address to The Australian Bar Association Bicentennial Conference, 11 July 1988.

Many of these rights and freedoms are similar to those in the European Convention. There are, in addition, two broadly worded provisions that I wish to mention again shortly. These are in sections 7 and 15. Section 7 provides:

Everyone has the right to life, liberty and security of person and the right not to be deprived thereof except in accordance with the principles of fundamental justice.

Section 15 is as follows:

(1) Every individual is equal before and under the law and has the right to the equal protection and the equal benefit of the law without discrimination and, in particular, without discrimination based on race, national or ethnic origin, colour, religion, sex, age or mental or physical disabilities.

(2) Subsection (1) does not preclude any law, programme or activity that has as its object the amelioration of conditions of disadvantaged individuals or groups, including those that are disadvantaged because of race, national or ethnic origin, colour, religion, sex, age or mental or physical disability.

It seems clear that the grounds of disability referred to in section 15 are not intended to be exhaustive.

In the United States Constitution the freedoms granted are set out in an absolute and unqualified manner. It is of course accepted by the courts that no freedom can be unqualified and that in any particular case it must be weighed against other social interests. The European Convention, on the other hand, prescribes express and varying limitations to many of the rights granted. For example, freedom of thought, conscience, and religion (article 9) can be limited by law in so far as the limitation is necessary in a democratic society in the interests of 'public safety, the protection of public order, health or morals, or for the protection of the rights and freedoms of others'. On the other hand, the right of freedom of expression (article 10) is subject to the same limitations and, in addition, to those that are necessary in the interests of 'national security', 'territorial integrity', 'the prevention of disorder or crime', the protection of 'reputation', 'preventing the disclosure of information received in confidence', and 'maintaining the authority and impartiality of the judiciary'.

In contrast to both the United States and the European position, the Canadian Charter has one general limitation clause which is in section 1 and is as follows:

The Canadian Charter of Rights and Freedoms guarantees the rights and freedoms set out in it subject only to such reasonable limits prescribed by law as can be demonstrably justified in a free and democratic society.

This provision does not suffer from the defects I discussed in relation to the views of Chief Justice Street and Justice Murphy, which require in effect that all laws be suitable for a free and democratic society. The application of this provision requires that one must first find a breach of an express guarantee. That is not to deny that it leaves a great deal to judicial creativity; but that situation is inevitable with any conceivable provision that is aimed at ensuring that an entrenched freedom is not regarded as absolute. It is intended as the anvil on which the judges would have to forge the necessary modifications of the enunciated rights and freedoms.

The Canadian Supreme Court has held that, whereas the onus of establishing a prima-facie violation of the Charter lies on the complainant, the onus of establishing the applicability of section 1 falls on the party (usually the Government) relying on that section.[50] This may require the submission of

[50] *R v Big M Drug Mart Ltd* (1985) 18 Dominion Law Report (4th) 621; *Hunter v Southam Inc.* (1984) 11 Dominion Law Reports (4th) 641.

evidence relating to broad social facts, including information of the sort associated with the 'Brandeis brief'.

A provision in the Canadian Charter that proved controversial in Australia among the members of the Constitutional Commission is known in Canada as the 'override clause'. Section 33 of the Charter permits a legislature expressly to declare in an Act that the Act or a provision of it shall operate notwithstanding many of the rights set out in the Charter. Such a declaration ceases to have effect after five years; but it may be continuously re-enacted for further five-year periods. The override clause does not apply to the political rights or to freedom of movement.

Section 33 may be seen as a compromise or adjustment of the interests of democratic responsible government and individual rights. It appears that this clause was adopted only because most of the Provinces would not otherwise have agreed to the Charter. The clause has been sparingly used. Quebec, which was the only Province not to approve the new constitutional settlement, attempted a wholesale provision applicable to all its previous legislation. It was held invalid by the Provincial court.[51] The Supreme Court held it valid except in so far as it purported to have a retrospective operation.[52] A few other specific override clauses have been enacted by the Quebec legislature.[53] In 1986 Saskatchewan became the second Province to use the override provision in relation to legislation to deal with a strike of government

[51] *Re. Alliance des Professeurs de Montreal and Attorney-General (Quebec)* (1985) 21 Dominion Law Reports (4th) 354.

[52] *Ford v Quebec (Attorney-General)* (1988) 54 Dominion Law Reports (4th) 577. The Act was not re-enacted by Quebec and thus ceased to be in force five years after its enactment on 23 June 1982.

[53] G. A. Beaudoin and E. Ratuskny (1989) *The Canadian Charter of Rights and Freedoms* 2nd edn, Carswell, Toronto, 108, n. 120.

employees. It proved unnecessary, as the Court held that the Act was not contrary to the Charter.[54]

In 1985, the New Zealand Government presented a White Paper on a Bill of Rights for New Zealand, hoping to achieve a general consensus. The draft Bill expressly declares that the Bill of Rights is the supreme law of New Zealand. Any law, including existing law, that is inconsistent with it is of no effect (section 1). It provides that no provision of the Bill can be amended or repealed except either by a majority of 75 per cent of members of the Parliament in a measure which expressly declares that it repeals or otherwise affects the Bill of Rights, or with the approval of a majority of voters at a referendum (section 28).

The New Zealand Bill was greatly influenced by the Canadian Charter. It contains a general limitations clause in the same terms, but has no override provision. Some of the more important deviations from the Canadian model are:

(a) It qualifies freedom of association by declaring that the right to form and join trade unions is consistent with 'legislative measures enacted to ensure effective trade union representation and to encourage orderly industrial relations'.

(b) There is no general equality provision, but simply freedom from discrimination on specified grounds. There is no express affirmative action provision (because the White Paper said that such action would not be regarded as discrimination).

(c) Section 7 of the Canadian Charter (relating to life, liberty, and security) is considerably reduced in scope in its New Zealand form and confined to the right to life. Section 14 of the New Zealand Bill provides:

[54] *Saskatchewan v RWDS Union* [1988] 1 Supreme Court Reports 460.

No one shall be deprived of life except on such grounds, and where applicable, in accordance with such procedures, as are established by law and are consistent with principles of fundamental justice.

In 1988 the Australian Constitutional Commission recommended that the existing rights against federal authorities – namely trial by jury, 'just terms' for the acquisition of property, and freedom of religion – be strengthened and extended to cover action by the States and Territories. This recommendation was one of four proposals that was the subject of a referendum on 3 September 1988. Another referendum proposal that was recommended by the Commission was the entrenchment of the principle of one vote–one value. It would have allowed only a 10 per cent deviation among the number of voters in any electorate. All the referendum proposals were defeated.

The more important recommendations on the issue of individual rights were not released until after the referendum. The Commission recommended the addition to the Constitution of a new chapter on rights and freedoms. The debt owed to the Canadian Charter and the New Zealand Bill is obvious. The substantive and criminal procedural rights are very similar to those in the other two instruments.

As in the case of New Zealand, a general equality clause was avoided and a right of freedom from discrimination on specified grounds was preferred. However, the Canadian model was followed to the extent that there is an express provision that the anti-discrimination clause is not infringed by measures to overcome disadvantages arising from various grounds such as race, sex, and so on. There is no general clause guaranteeing life, liberty, or security of person and no reference to 'principles of fundamental justice'.

The Australian Constitutional Commission, while unanimous on everything else regarding rights and freedoms, was split three to two on the value of the Canadian provision called the 'override clause'. Ironically, the majority who were against it were a former Labor Prime Minister (Mr Whitlam) and a former Liberal Premier of Victoria (Sir Rupert Hamer). The third member of the majority was the Chairman, Sir Maurice Byers, a former Federal Solicitor-General. Professor Enid Campbell of Monash University and I were in the minority. Like the Canadians, however, we did not wish to extend the power to opt out to cover provisions relating to democratic freedoms, such as the right to vote and the value of the vote.

The majority considered an override clause to be wrong in principle. Parliament should not be able, by simple Act, to override rights that are intended as protection for the minority against the Parliament and the Government. Freedoms, they said, need protection when most under challenge.[55] They are most under challenge at a time when those in need of such protection are the targets of anger or hysteria. It is at such times that the elected representatives are likely to either share or feel overborne by the errors of the electorate, and so remove the shield of entrenched constitutional freedoms. It was their view, therefore, that, if Governments have good reasons for promoting legislation which limits guaranteed freedom, they should be prepared to demonstrate to a court that it is justifiable.

The minority were concerned to propose a regime for constitutional protection of rights and, at the same time, meet objections that the courts should not have the last word on many difficult social issues which would require a referen-

[55] *Final Report of the Constitutional Commission* (1988) para 9.226, Australian Government Publishing Service, Canberra.

dum of the people to change. It is extremely likely in Australia, as in Canada, that Governments will find it politically difficult to state expressly in legislation that they wish to push aside constitutional rights and freedoms or overturn High Court decisions declaring certain rights to be included in the constitutional guarantees. What the minority proposed was really an extension to legislation of what has happened in relation to administrative and executive decisions.

Theoretically, it is open to Parliament to say clearly and expressly that it is giving power to a person to make decisions that are *mala fide*, for wrongful purposes, and in accordance with unfair procedures. It is, however, not politically easy. A constitutional provision relating to rights, coupled with an override clause, would extend this state of affairs to parliamentary legislation. If, in a time of social passion, Parliament was prepared expressly to override constitutional rights, it would be required (under our proposals) to repeat the process at three-yearly intervals.

A common argument against a Bill of Rights in all the four countries is, or has been, that our judges are not equipped for such tasks. It is of course clear that the effective interpretation and application of a Bill of Rights involves a capacity to examine and adjust conflicting social interests, to examine factual social data, and, on a more general plane, to consider in a sophisticated way the relationship of the judiciary to the democratic arms of government. Much therefore depends on the ability, the quality, and the professional outlook of the judiciary. Until recent times the decisions of the High Court of Australia and the Supreme Court of Canada in relation to analogous matters did not give much cause for optimism. The same is true of a number of decisions of British courts.

As mentioned above, the Australian Constitution contains

a few provisions that are in the nature of individual rights. Section 116 provides among other things that the Commonwealth shall not make any law 'for prohibiting the free exercise of any religion'. In *Krygger v Williams*[56] it was held that a law for compulsory military training as applied to a person whose religion forbad him to take part in military activities was not in breach of this provision. Military training was said to have 'nothing at all to do with religion'. In *Adelaide Company of Jehovah's Witnesses Inc v Commonwealth*[57] it was held that section 116 did not preclude laws dissolving a religious group and prohibiting the advocacy of doctrines or principles which, although advocated in pursuance of religious convictions, were prejudicial to the prosecution of the war. There is some irony in the fact that a number of the provisions were held invalid on the ground that the interference with property rights went beyond what was permitted under the defence power. All the judges, however, recognized that section 116 required balancing religious freedom with other social interests; but several adopted broad criteria to describe the qualifications on such freedom, including 'unsocial actions' (at 155), 'subversive' (at 149), contrary to 'social order' and 'dangerous to the common weal' (at 150). Latham CJ gave a more detailed analysis, but determined the matter on the basis that religious freedom was qualified by the continuance of the organized community (at 131–2).

An even narrower approach was adopted in relation to section 117 of the Constitution which provides as follows: 'A subject of the Queen, resident in any State, shall not be subject in any other State to any disability or discrimination

[56] (1912) 15 Commonwealth Law Reports 366.
[57] (1943) 67 Commonwealth Law Reports 116.

which would not be equally applicable to him if he were a subject of the Queen resident in such other State'. In 1973 a majority of the Court upheld South Australian admission rules for legal practitioners which required a period of residence in South Australia for admission. The judges said that the rules did not breach section 117 because all persons, whether permanently resident in South Australia or not, had to satisfy the residential requirements. This is hardly the finest form of judicial policy-making and craftsmanship. If a provision designed to ensure equality of treatment for all citizens could be so easily evaded one wonders why it was in the Constitution at all.[58]

In the last few years, however, there has been a change of attitude by judges of the High Court in relation to many aspects of the Constitution. There is a movement away from creating and relying on formal criteria and technical formulae; more emphasis is placed on divining the purpose of the provision, and looking at more practical and factual matters in the interpretation and application of constitutional provisions. This is illustrated by a case decided in 1989, when the 1973 decision referred to above was overruled. The Court emphasized that the effect of any law on the individual had to be examined as a matter of fact. The Court held that section 117 prevented Queensland from denying a New South Wales lawyer a right of practice in Queensland on the sole ground that his residence or principal place of business was not in Queensland. In reaching this decision section 117 was construed as a provision both protecting the individual and promoting national cohesion and the establishment of a national citizenship.[59] If this trend should continue, the

[58] *Henry v Boehm* (1973) 128 Commonwealth Law Reports 482.
[59] *Street v Queensland Bar Association* (1989) 88 Australian Law Reports 321.

arguments which have been made against a Bill of Rights for Australia on the ground that the judges cannot be trusted to interpret and apply them in a sensible manner will be effectively answered.

The same argument relating to the inadequacies of the judiciary was made in Canada, where judicial experience also provided justification for that view. The history of interpretation of the Canadian Bill of Rights of 1960 – a federal statute – did not give anyone confidence that the Canadian courts were capable of adequately deciding disputes about entrenched constitutional rights. This Act is applicable only to federal laws. Although it has in large part been superseded by the Charter of Rights, it has not been repealed. The Act declares the existence and continuation of a number of rights 'without discrimination by reason of race, national origin, colour, religion, or sex'. Section 2 generally provides that any Act shall be construed and applied so as not to infringe those rights 'unless it is expressly declared by an Act . . . that it shall operate notwithstanding' the Bill of Rights. It took ten years and a number of cases before the Supreme Court decided that the Bill of Rights was not a mere rule of construction,[60] when the Court held inoperative a provision (enacted before the Bill of Rights) making it an offence for an Indian, but not anyone who was not an Indian, to be intoxicated in a non-public place. This remains the only substantive enactment to be deprived of operation as a result of inconsistency with the Bill of Rights. Later cases, it has been said, 'emasculated' the Bill of Rights. Dickson CJ in 1985 referred to the view that 'the Canadian judiciary were indecisive and unadventurous' when dealing

[60] *R v Drybones* [1970] Supreme Court Reports 282.

with it.[61] The prohibition against discrimination was regarded as aimed merely at 'the administration and the enforcement of the law by ordinary courts'.[62] It was also said that discrimination could be justified on the ground that it had the purpose of achieving 'a valid federal objective'.[63] It was not clear whether there was any difference between this test and the issue whether the law was valid under the distribution of powers in the *Constitution Act*.[64] One writer suggested that the inability of the Court to deal with a Bill of Rights was rooted in Canadian culture.[65]

Despite a certain foreboding, based on past experience, the Canadian Supreme Court has tackled the interpretation of the Canadian Charter of Rights and Freedoms in an entirely different spirit. The fact that the provisions are part of the Constitution and difficult to amend seems to have made a great difference in judicial attitudes. It appears also that the manner of creating a Bill or Charter of Rights, together with social expectations and community consensus, contribute to judicial approaches to interpretation in this area. Whatever the reasons, the Canadian judiciary has assumed what has been called 'an overtly activist posture'. The judges have insisted on giving a liberal and generous interpretation to the rights granted. As I have mentioned, the onus is on the Government to prove that an infringement of a right is both reasonable and demonstrably justifiable in

[61] N. Finkelstein (1986) *Laskin's Canadian Constitutional Law*, 5th edn, Vol. 2, Carswell, Toronto, 998.
[62] *Bliss v Attorney General* (Canada) [1979] 1 Supreme Court Reports 183.
[63] *R v Burnshine* [1975] 1 Supreme Court Reports 693.
[64] N. Finkelstein (1986) *Laskin's Canadian Constitutional Law*, 5th edn, Vol. 2, Carswell, Toronto, 994–5.
[65] Gold, 'Equality Before the Law in the Supreme Court of Canada: A Case Study' (1980) 18 *Osgoode Hall Law Journal* 336.

a free and democratic community. This is treated as an exception to the freedom and to be construed (unlike the rights and freedoms) strictly. The standard of proof must be applied 'vigorously', and the social concerns involved must be 'pressing and substantial'.[66] The enunciation of these principles distinguishes the approach of the Court today from that of pre-Charter days; but it has not avoided the interest balancing and judicial policy-making role inherent in the judicial task of applying entrenched rights.

In only seven years there has been produced a great many cases and vast literature. A political scientist in 1988 estimated that there had been about 500 cases before all Canadian courts each year which involved the Charter. To the middle of 1988 the Supreme Court had dealt with about fifty such cases.[67] Most of these related to the criminal justice system and other procedural provisions, which many would regard as being most appropriately the function of judges – an area with which they are most familiar. Most of these cases do not involve the validity of legislation but concern the actions of the police and courts. But even in this area – matters such as arrest, search, confessions, onus of proof, and statutory presumptions – the Canadian Supreme Court has, in the words of Sir Anthony Mason, the Chief Justice of Australia, 'moved well beyond the reach of the common law'.[68]

Whatever one may think of decisions in this field, there are other politically contentious areas which more clearly evidence the social policy-making role of judges in interpreting entrenched rights. Is the right to strike an ingredient of

[66] *R v Oakes* [1986] 1 Supreme Court Reports 103.
[67] Peter H. Russell, 'Canada's Charter of Rights and Freedoms: A Political Report' [1986] *Public Law* 385–6.
[68] A. Mason, supra n. 36.

freedom of association? The majority said 'No'. A minority said 'Yes'.[69] The case raised many policy issues, including, of course, the role of the Court. Some of the majority judges were concerned that a court was not fitted to determine in each case whether a particular legislative restriction in this area came within the scope of section 1 of the Charter. Also, if the right to pursue the activities of the association was within the guarantee of freedom of association, that would open up for judicial review a wide variety of controls of business and commercial associations. The dissenting judges (Dickson CJ and Wilson J) met the problem by emphasizing the need for associations to protect and enhance the interests of those who otherwise lacked power and influence equal to those with whom their interests interacted or conflicted, such as minorities and workers.

Many politically contentious issues have arisen, or have the potential to arise, under the two provisions that the Australian and New Zealand bodies refused to follow. The prohibition of abortion, except under tough and strict legislative conditions, was held by a majority to be contrary to section 7 guaranteeing 'life, liberty, and security'.[70]

In respect of section 7 the right not to be deprived of life, liberty, or security except in accordance with the principles of fundamental justice – there is evidence that the framers intended to avoid issues of 'substantive due process' in the American sense. The phrase 'due process of law' was deliberately omitted. Officials advised that the provision was aimed

---

[69] *Reference re. Public Service Employee Relations Act* (Alberta) [1987] 1 Supreme Court Reports 313; *Public Service Alliance of Canada v The Queen* [1987] 1 Supreme Court Reports 424; *RWDS Union v Saskatchewan* [1987] 1 Supreme Court Reports 460.

[70] *Morgentaler v The Queen* [1988] 1 Supreme Court Reports 30.

at ensuring procedural justice.[71] The Court has held otherwise.[72] They have held it is up to the courts to determine whether liberty has been impaired unjustly in the substantive sense. This, together with defining what is 'liberty' and 'security', opens up wide policy issues of the sort I raised previously regarding political ideology and economic policy. This is why the Australian and New Zealand bodies decided to avoid the provision. (If, as suggested, procedural fairness was all that was intended, the drafting of the provision, with its reference to fundamental justice, left much to be desired.)

After vigorous assertions of the right of the individual as against the State in the earlier years, the Court has shown in more recent times that it is conscious of these problems. There is more awareness that the issue may involve balancing the interests of those adversely affected by the legislation and those who benefit from it. The Chief Justice has said:

> In interpreting and applying the Charter I believe that the courts must be cautious to ensure that it does not become an instrument of better situated individuals to roll back legislation which has as its object the improvement of the condition of less advantaged persons.[73]

It has also been said that the principles of fundamental justice are to be sought in 'the basic tenets of our legal system', not 'in the realm of general public policy but in the inherent domain of the judiciary as guardians of the judicial system'.[74] The elusiveness of this distinction needs no elabo-

---

[71] *Weatherall v Attorney-General (Canada)* (1987) 11 Federal Trial Reports 279, 288–91.
[72] *Re. B C Motor Vehicle Act* [1985] 2 Supreme Court Reports 486; *Vaillancourt v The Queen* [1987] 2 Supreme Court Reports 636.
[73] *Edwards Books and Arts Ltd v The Queen* [1986] 2 Supreme Court Reports 713, 779.
[74] *Re. B C Motor Vehicle Act* [1985] 2 Supreme Court Reports 486, 503.

ration. As Mr Justice Strayer has put it: '(O)ne judge's basic tenet may be another's transitory aberration.'[75] It may be that an override clause may make judges less concerned about activism. In reply to the argument that the judicial review of legislation is undemocratic, a court can always reply that it is open to Parliament to change the situation.

The other provision that can be a fruitful ground of litigation is the equality section. A general guarantee of equality gives no guidance to the court. Practically every law treats people differently, from criminal law to taxation law. Whether it treats like cases alike and unlike cases differently will, under section 15 of the Charter, depend on the view of the judge, unhelped by the Charter, as to whether the difference is based on relevant or arbitrary criteria. The New Zealand White Paper quotes Professor Peter Hogg as saying of the Canadian provision that it has the potential to be the most intrusive provision of the Charter and that it is very difficult to give a confident opinion whether any given law would be secure.[76] McIntyre J of the Canadian Supreme Court has said that 'it is an elusive concept and, more than any of the other rights and freedoms guaranteed in the Charter, it lacks precise definition'.[77]

In *Andrews v Law Society of British Columbia*[78] the Supreme Court made its first attempt at a general elucidation of section 15. The judges held unanimously that a requirement of Canadian citizenship for admission to the Bar of British Columbia infringed or denied equality rights in section 15,

---

[75] B. L. Strayer, 'Life under the Canadian Charter: Adjusting the Balance between Legislatures and Courts' [1988] *Public Law* 347, 368.
[76] *A Bill of Rights for New Zealand: A White Paper* (1985) 86–7, para 10.82, Government Printer, Wellington.
[77] [1989] 1 Supreme Court Reports 143 at 164.
[78] [1989] 1 Supreme Court Reports 143.

and, by a majority, that it was not justified under section 1 of the Charter. The Court rejected the view that section 15 required all distinctions between individuals or groups to be justified under section 1. They accepted that the grounds of discrimination enumerated were not exhaustive, so that grounds 'analogous' to those enumerated were covered; but they left open the question whether the section had even broader coverage. Generally speaking, distinctions based on 'personal characteristics' will be caught by section 15; 'while those based on an individual's merits and capacities will rarely be so classed'.[79] As section 15 is not regarded as covering all differences of treatment, the relationship between section 15 and section 1 is – as the Court recognized – extremely difficult; yet it is of great practical importance because of the difference in onus of proof under the two provisions.

I have avoided the issue of how countries like New Zealand and the United Kingdom entrench a Bill of Rights. The issue of parliamentary sovereignty – whether it is continuing or self-embracing, whether Parliament may redefine itself or its manner and form of making laws – has been examined extensively over many decades. Nothing I add to the debate would be novel. Yet, as I mentioned earlier, outsiders such as Australians see Britain in practical terms as having something in the nature of a Bill of Rights that is interpreted and applied by foreigners. Its procedures may, from the individual point of view, be highly inefficient, but the decisions, generally speaking, seem to be accepted. Laws and executive actions are judged against an instrument declaring such rights. This goes beyond anything Australia or New Zealand have. It passes my understanding

[79] *Ibid.* 174–5.

why the British do not see the virtue of having such questions determined by their own courts, initially at least.

It seems now unlikely that the proposed Bill of Rights as a basic constitutional instrument will materialize in New Zealand. The White Paper was referred to a Parliamentary Committee which presented its final report in 1988.[80] A majority of the Committee recommended that a Bill of Rights should be enacted 'as an ordinary statute, that is, not as supreme law and not entrenched'. The Bill 'would provide guidance to the judiciary in interpreting legislation, making it plain that interpretations consistent with the rights set out in the Bill were to be adopted'. It may be that the proposed law will be something like the Canadian Bill of Rights of 1960. Its ultimate effect will depend, of course, on the wording of such a law; but it will depend just as much on the attitude of the judges. As indicated above, the evidence is that the Canadian legislation had little bite, but the temper of the times may now be different. We have the extra-judicial statement of Sir Robin Cooke that 'in the 1980s a New Zealand Bill might be in somewhat similar terms, but it would be launched into a very different climate of opinion. It might be much more effective.'[81]

As a result of the recent referendum, it is unlikely that the recommendations of the Australian Constitutional Commission will, in the immediate future, be put to the people. It might be, therefore, that Australia could be even more isolated in this area of legal endeavour than Sir Anthony Mason suggested.

Whatever may be the fate in the short term of proposals

---

[80] *Final Report of the Justice and Law Reform Committee on a White Paper on a Bill of Rights for New Zealand* (1988) Government Printer, Wellington.

[81] R. Cooke, 'Fundamentals', A paper delivered to the First Canada–Australia Law Conference [1988] *New Zealand Law Journal* 158, 159.

for entrenched rights in the United Kingdom, Australia, and New Zealand, it is difficult to believe that that would be the end of the story. There is considerable and continuing dissatisfaction, at least among a substantial minority, as to the operation of parliamentary democracy in all these countries. Many old shibboleths are being questioned. The common law is no longer regarded by all as a sufficient protection of individual rights. This is true of some British judges. Lord Bridge, in his dissenting judgement in the first *Spycatcher case*, said:

> We have not adopted as part of our law the European Convention for the Protection of Human Rights and Fundamental Freedoms to which this country is a signatory. Many think that we should. I have hitherto not been of that persuasion, in large part because I have had confidence in the capacity of the common law to safeguard the fundamental freedoms essential to a free society, including the right to freedom of speech which is specifically safeguarded by article 10 of the Convention. My confidence is seriously undermined by your Lordships' decision.[82]

It might be argued that, if Lord Bridge is correct, a Bill of Rights will not help because the same judges would be interpreting it as were interpreting the common law. The Canadian experience shows, however, that a different judicial attitude can result if an instrument has general concurrence and is regarded as incorporating principles of basic importance.

One thing is clear. The old complacency about individual liberty, in our communities, has gone.

---

[82] *Attorney-General v 'The Guardian'* [1987] 1 Weekly Law Reports 1248 at 1286.

3

FEDERAL AND SUPRA-NATIONAL FEATURES

The British Parliament has been the creator of many federal systems, some of which failed and some of which were successful. Those of Canada and Australia have been long-term successes. The Canadian system has operated over 120 years and that of Australia for nearly ninety years. In the world, only the United States and Swiss federal systems can boast of similar or greater longevity. Yet traditionally the British have had a considerable disdain for federalism. Again Dicey must be mentioned as a prominent influence in furthering this attitude. He referred, in 1915, to a then new but brief interest in converting the United Kingdom into a federal state. He said this object was a 'delusion' which was 'absolutely foreign to the historical and, so to speak, instinctive policy of English constitutionalists'.[1]

The Royal Commission on the (British) Constitution in their report in 1973 concluded that the demands of modern government and the inevitable financial strength of central federal Governments had undermined regional sovereignty in all federations. Indeed they said that 'what is actually in

[1] A. V. Dicey (1915) *The Law and the Constitution*, 8th edn, Macmillan, xc; D. G. T. Williams, 'The Constituion of the United Kingdom' (1972) *Cambridge Law Journal* 266.

operation is not true federalism'. They admitted that this picture did not fit Canada, where Provincial sovereignty was strong. In any case, the Commissioners were of the view that a formal division of powers slowed down desirable changes or could prevent them altogether.

The strong provincial sovereignty of Canada, they said, was hardly a 'convenient' system and 'made things difficult'. Provincial sovereignty was no longer a realistic concept. They further declared that in the United States and in Canada, for example, the constitutional division of sovereignty had made it difficult to achieve the kind of system the people 'really need'.[2]

It is not necessary to agree or disagree with the Commission's view that the United Kingdom should not be a federal state to find this statement either puzzling or arrogant. Whether or not the people of, say, the United States, Canada, Australia, or Switzerland 'really *need*' a federal system, it is clear that, generally, most of them really *want* what they have. There is not any hope that they would vote to have a unitary state modelled on that of the United Kingdom. As to whether what they have is 'true federalism', that opens up broad issues, both conceptual and functional, which the Royal Commission's report did not investigate. If the four countries I have mentioned are not true federations, there is none in the world. Yet they clearly have characteristics in common which distinguish them from, say, Britain, New Zealand, or Denmark. It is, for example, of great significance that the federal Parliament of Australia cannot abolish the governmental structure of Queensland, as the

---

[2] *Report of the Royal Commission on the Constitution* (1973) Command Paper 5460 para 513–23.

British Parliament has done with that of Northern Ireland and of Greater London.

While writers and scholars differ as to the countries they would place under the rubric of true or classic federations, all lists include Canada and Australia. Yet, while the constitutional framers in both countries desired an entrenched division of legislative and executive powers among a central and regional Government, they differed in their aims as to the strength of power to be given to the central authorities and to be retained by the regions. As a result of judicial construction the framers' objects were probably not fulfilled, and their assumptions were certainly not borne out, in either country.

It is clear that the Quebec Resolutions, on which the *British North America Act* was based, aimed at a strongly centralized federation. There was a belief that one of the factors that caused the United States Civil War (recently concluded) was the weakness of the federal Government and, in particular, the retention by the States of all residuary power.[3]

The Canadian plan was to confer limited exclusive power on the Provinces, leaving all the residue to the federal Government. The Canadian Parliament was empowered in section 91 to make laws for the peace, order, and good government of Canada in relation to all matters not coming within exclusive Provincial power. A list of specified exclusive federal powers was set out, but the section declared that this was 'for greater certainty and not so as to restrict the generality of the foregoing terms of this section'. A separate

---

[3] W. P. M. Kennedy (1930) *Statutes, Treaties and Documents of the Canadian Constitution*, 2nd edn, Oxford University Press, Toronto, 558–9.

provision (section 132) empowered the federal Parliament to give legislative effect to treaty obligations.

Section 92 then gave exclusive legislative power to the Provinces, which at first sight appears quite limited in scope. It includes such matters as the establishment and maintenance of prisons, hospitals, and charities; shop, saloon, tavern, and auctioneer licences; the solemnization of marriage; local works; and municipal institutions. One subject however proved to be of enormous importance, namely, 'Property and civil rights in the Province'. Exclusive power over education (subject to conditions) was granted by section 93. Nevertheless, on reading the *British North America Act* (now the *Canadian Constitution Act*) for the first time, and free of all knowledge of later constitutional development, one sees a resemblance between the powers of the Provinces and the powers of local government bodies in some countries. The supreme position of the central authority was confirmed by Part V of the Act, which empowered the Governor-General to appoint and recall Lieutenant-Governors of the Provinces and to disallow Provincial legislation.

When the Australian colonies were considering federation in the 1890s they quickly rejected the Canadian model. Many of the delegates considered that the Canadian Constitution resembled a unified rather than a federal one. They wished their federal Government and Parliament to have only those specific powers that were expressly granted to it. Otherwise the States were to retain all their pre-existing powers. Even in relation to most federal subjects the States retained concurrent power to make laws, subject to being superseded by any inconsistent federal law.

This contrasted with the Canadian attempt to divide up the world (except for agriculture and immigration) into two exclusive zones of power. It would also have been quite unthinkable for the Australian delegates to have contemplated giving the Australian government the power to disallow State legislation or to appoint State Governors.

Apart from marriage and divorce, the powers of the Commonwealth are concerned primarily with public or commercial matters. It was intended that the vast bulk of laws, particularly those related to the day-to-day life of the individual, would remain exclusively within State power. The Australians generally favoured, in its federal features, the American Constitution. For example, whereas the Canadian Parliament was given express exclusive power to make laws regulating trade and commerce, the Australian Parliament's power (following the United States example) was limited to inter-state and overseas trade and commerce.

Since their enactments, the provisions of the Canadian and Australian Constitutions, in relation to the distribution of powers, have not in form changed significantly. Yet, as a result of judicial construction, the Canadian Provinces are more powerful and the central Government weaker than (I think) in any other federation. By the same judicial means, the power of Australian central government has grown and continues to grow, while that of the States has waned, to a degree that would have astonished the framers.

Until 1949 the interpretation of the Canadian Constitution was largely in the hands of the Judicial Committee of the Privy Council. In that period the Canadian framework of government was moulded by that body to a shape that is still recognizable today (although I find it difficult to discern in the document itself). Lord Watson, followed by Lord Haldane, had a constitutional vision of a federal balance which required the Provinces to have exclusive control of all domestic matters in the absence of any clear indication to the contrary. They achieved this by making the exclusive Provincial power to make laws in relation to 'Property and civil rights in the Province', the centre of the entire system.

It was necessary in their view to reconcile this power with specific exclusive powers granted to the federal Parliament, such as those relating to trade and commerce, criminal law, banking, etc. Despite the clear intention to confer federal power over all trade and commerce, the Privy Council declared that, as it was necessary to prevent overlapping between that power and the Provincial power over property and civil rights, the federal power must be, generally speaking, confined to inter-Provincial and overseas commerce. This reduced the power, by means of implication, to the scope of the subject matter of the United States and the later Australian provision.[4] It was held therefore that insurance was a Provincial and not a federal matter.[5] If a particular act of trade, business, or industry was local, the fact that commercial activity or business was organized on national lines or that an industry was spread throughout the country did not bring it within federal power to control. Federal Acts prohibiting monopolies, controlling prices, regulating labour relations, and licensing grain elevators in respect of wheat (most of which was exported from a Province) were all held invalid.[6]

All these matters, their Lordships said, dealt with local trade or local works. The economic effect on matters within federal power was treated as irrelevant.

In 1881, in *Citizens Insurance v Parsons*,[7] the Privy Council

[4] *Citizens' Insurance Co. v Parsons* (1881) 7 Appeal Cases 96.
[5] *Insurance Reference* case [1916] Appeal Cases 348.
[6] *Board of Commerce* case [1922] 1 Appeal Cases 191; *Toronto Electric Commissioners v Snider* [1925] Appeal Cases 396; *The King v Eastern Terminal Elevator Co.* [1925] 3 Dominion Law Reports 1.
[7] (1881) 7 Appeal Cases 96.

FEDERAL AND SUPRA-NATIONAL FEATURES

suggested, in cautious terms, that the trade and commerce power would extend to 'general regulation of trade affecting the whole Dominion', but it was later made clear that this was a very narrow category. The Privy Council rejected the view that the Parliament could regulate insurance because it was a business spread throughout the country without regard to Provincial boundaries.[8] In 1989 the Canadian Chief Justice referred to the 'general trade' aspect of the power as *'terra incognita'*. He could find only two occasions in over a century when legislation was upheld on that ground.[9]

I mentioned that the specific powers given to the Canadian Parliament were stated as examples of subjects that came within the general power to make laws for the peace, order, and good government of Canada. In the hands of Lord Haldane this power was declared to be confined to national emergencies which could be no more than temporary, such as war.[10] The federal residuary power, which the framers thought so important, seemed to have disappeared. Provincial power over property and civil rights became in effect the residuary power. The intended central thrust of Canadian federalism, which the Australians had disliked so much, had been judicially turned in precisely the opposite direction. Almost anything could be regarded as property and civil rights in the Province.

For a few years, after the death of Lord Haldane in 1928, there occurred an aberrant period when it seemed that the

---

[8] [1916] 1 Appeal Cases 588.
[9] *General Motors of Canada Ltd v City National Leasing* [1989] 1 Supreme Court Reports 641, 657.
[10] *Fort Frances Pulp and Power Co. Ltd v Manitoba Free Press Co. Ltd* [1923] Appeal Cases 695.

Privy Council would change its approach. Under Lord Sankey there was emphasized the notion of a constitution as an organism which must adjust to changing circumstances. He declared that 'the British North America Act planted in Canada a living tree capable of growth and expansion within its natural limits'.[11] It was held that all air navigation and broadcasting were within federal power on several grounds. The laws in part gave effect to international conventions, they came within the residuary power because of their national dimensions, and, in the case of broadcasting, came within the enumerated power over 'telegraphs'.[12] It was declared that 'in interpreting a constituent or organic statute ... that construction most beneficial to the widest possible amplitude of its powers must be adopted'.[13]

This new approach occurred just before the United States Supreme Court executed its constitutional *volte face* at the beginning of President Roosevelt's second term, inaugurating a great expansion of national power over the economy. In Canada the exact opposite occurred. Lord Atkin, replacing Lord Sankey as chief constitutional interpreter, narrowly construed the earlier decisions and reverted to the earlier Haldane approach. The Canadian 'new deal' legislation, providing for minimum wages, maximum hours of work, social insurance, etc., was held invalid on the grounds that the provisions had to be characterized as relating to property and civil rights. The federal residuary power was again confined to emergencies, which did not include a long-term

---

[11] *Edwards v Attorney-General (Canada)* [1930] Appeal Cases 124, 136.
[12] *Re. Regulation and Control of Aeronautics in Canada* [1932] Appeal Cases 54; *Re. Regulation and Control of Radio Communications in Canada* [1932] Appeal Cases 304.
[13] *British Coal Corporation v The King* [1935] Appeal Cases 500, 518.

economic and social malaise, such as the world economic depression.[14]

It was argued that some of this legislation was made in pursuance of an international convention binding Canada. Section 132 gave the Parliament and Government of Canada 'all powers necessary or proper for performing the Obligations of Canada or of any Province thereof, as Part of the British Empire, towards Foreign Countries, arising under Treaties between the Empire and such Foreign Countries'. Their Lordships held that this provision was inapplicable because the relevant treaty was not one that Great Britain had entered into on behalf of the countries of the Empire. It had been entered into by Canada as a sovereign state. The conclusion was that as a result of Canada acquiring independence, and therefore international personality, it had lost a legislative power that it had while it was a colony. In place of Sankey's 'living tree', Lord Atkin substituted the following metaphoric utterance: 'While the ship of state now sails on larger ventures and into foreign waters she still retains the watertight compartments which are an essential part of her original structure.'[15]

From 1949 the Privy Council ceased to control the development of Canadian constitutional law. The Supreme Court of Canada became the final interpreter. Despite several decades of often bitter criticism by Canadian constitutional lawyers of the earlier decisions,[16] no sudden revolu-

[14] *Attorney-General (Canada) v Attorney-General (Ontario)* [1937] Appeal Cases 326 and 355.
[15] *Ibid.*, 354.
[16] For example, F. R. Scott, 'The Consequences of the Privy Council Decisions' (1937) 15 *Canadian Bar Review* 485; V. C. Macdonald, 'The Privy Council and the Canadian Constitution' (1951) 29 *Canadian Bar Review* 1021; W. P. M. Kennedy, 'The Interpretation of the British North America Act' (1943) 8 *Cambridge Law Journal* 146.

tion occurred. Indeed none could have been expected. Canadian political and economic affairs, inter-governmental arrangements, and general expectations had for eighty years been made in accordance with existing constitutional assumptions. Also, a new generation of Canadian legal, political, and constitutional scholars began to look more kindly upon the earlier work of the Privy Council. It was suggested that, whatever may have been the intention of the framers, the decisions reflected the centrifugal forces in Canadian society.[17] It was questioned whether Canada would have survived as a unity if the judiciary had construed the Constitution in accordance with what appeared to many to be its original highly centralized object. This argument may ignore the fact that judicial decisions may not merely reflect social forces, but may in fact influence them.

However that may be, the Supreme Court has to a degree moved gradually towards a federal balance that is weighed more in favour of the central government. The general or residuary power has been held to include some matters of national concern including air navigation, the national capital, and offshore mineral resources.[18] The emergency aspect of that power (which as we noted was not applicable to the depression of the 1930s) was held to apply to the economic problem of the 1970s – high inflation and high unemployment. The Court upheld a federal law controlling income and prices for a limited period. It seems clear, however, that without the emergency the law would have

[17] For example, Alan C. Cairns, 'The Judicial Committee and its Critics' (1971) 4 *Canadian Journal of Political Science* 301.
[18] *Johannesson v West St Paul* [1952] 1 Supreme Court Reports 297; *Munro v National Capital Commission* [1966] Supreme Court Reports 663; *Re. Offshore Mineral Rights of British Columbia* [1967] Supreme Court Reports 792.

been invalid. The majority declared that to regard the mere control of inflation as a national matter would have threatened 'the equilibrium of the Constitution'.[19]

The Court has also adopted a more practical and flexible approach to determining the boundary between intra-Provincial commerce and inter-Provincial and overseas commerce. There is a tendency to look more at the practical effects on inter-Provincial and overseas trade, even though the law may operate directly on local matters.[20]

New life has been given to the 'general trade' aspect of the trade and commerce power. The Supreme Court in 1989, declared that the *Combines Investigation Act* was valid under that power.[21] Hitherto the control of monopolies and restrictive trade practices had been governed federally by means of the criminal law. From 1976, however, a civil remedy was added and a Restrictive Trade Practices Commission was given increased powers. In relying on the trade and commerce power the Court treated as relevant the fact that the nature of the legislation was such that it could not have been enacted by the Provinces jointly or severally, and that the failure to include one or more Provinces would have jeopardized the operation of the scheme elsewhere. To determine these questions the Court examined reports and studies of the actual operation of Canadian business and commerce.

---

[19] *Re. Anti-Inflation Act* [1976] 2 Supreme Court Reports 373.

[20] *Caloil Inc. v Attorney-General (Canada)* [1971] Supreme Court Reports 543; *Attorney-General (Manitoba) v Manitoba Egg and Poultry Association* [1971] Supreme Court Reports 689; *Central Canada Potash Co. Ltd v Saskatchewan* [1979] 1 Supreme Court Reports 42; *Re. Agricultural Products Marketing Act* [1978] 2 Supreme Court Reports 1198.

[21] *General Motors of Canada Ltd v City National Leasing* [1989] 1 Supreme Court Reports 641.

Nevertheless, the Court is cautious about expanding the operation of the power. There is no movement towards giving it a literal meaning, and so detracting considerably from Provincial power.[22] To come within the 'general trade' aspect it is regarded as relevant that the legislation is part of a general scheme and is not concerned with particular industries, but with 'trade as a whole'. The Chief Justice spoke of the need 'to maintain a delicate balance between federal and provincial power'. It seems to remain the case that in Canada the control of most businesses and trades, securities and insurance, and labour relations, remain within Provincial power; that is, the exclusive power of the Provinces to make laws with respect to property and civil rights.

In effect, the Canadian Supreme Court is still concerned with preserving a federal balance. It has simply shifted to some degree away from an earlier heavy emphasis on Provincial power. In adjusting the two sets of powers there seems to be a more functional and practical approach as distinct from the somewhat arbitrary and wooden dichotomies expounded in earlier times. Nevertheless, the basic principles developed by the Privy Council are plainly discernible.

The Privy Council had little to do with the distribution of powers under the Australian Constitution. Section 74 of the Constitution declared, among other things, that there should be no appeal from the High Court upon any question as to the limits *inter se* of the constitutional powers of the Commonwealth and the States, unless the High Court certified that it ought to be determined by the Privy Council. Only

---

[22] *McDonald v Vapor* [1977] 2 Supreme Court Reports 134; *Labatt Breweries v Attorney-General (Canada)* [1980] 1 Supreme Court Reports 914.

one certificate was ever granted, and that was in 1912.[23] All other applications have been refused. Like the Privy Council in respect of Canada, however, the High Court for the first seventeen years of its existence (1903 to 1920) read into the Constitution the image the majority had both of a federal state and the federal balance of power. On this occasion they may have been more in line with the assumptions of at least many of the founding fathers.

They accepted that the Australian Constitution was modelled on that of the United States in its federal features and took careful note of American decisions. They implied from the Constitution two doctrines. The first was that federalism required the Commonwealth and the States each to be free of interference and control by the other. It was held, therefore, that the States could not levy a tax on the income received by federal officials living in a State, and that the Commonwealth could not apply its compulsory industrial arbitration legislation to disputes between State governments and their railway employees. There was nothing expressly in the Constitution about this. The doctrine was regarded as necessarily implied in a federal constitution. Each government was 'sovereign' in its own sphere and therefore of necessity could not be hampered in its affairs by the other.[24]

The second doctrine was concerned with ensuring substantial State power. Although the Constitution does not list any subjects of State power, the early Court inferred from the limitation in the commerce power and from the other

---

[23] *Attorney-General (Cth) v Colonial Sugar Refining Co. Ltd* (1912) 17 Commonwealth Law Reports 644.

[24] *D'Emden v Pedder* (1904) 1 Commonwealth Law Reports 91; *Deakin v Webb* (1904) 1 Commonwealth Law Reports 585; *Railway Servants Case* (1906) 4 Commonwealth Law Reports 488.

powers given to the Commonwealth that the Constitution impliedly reserved to the States exclusive power over domestic affairs, in the absence of any clear indication to the contrary. This made applicable the Canadian technique of attempting to reconcile two different grants of power. As happened in Canada in relation to property and civil rights, the implied reserved power of the States over domestic affairs was treated as the major premise in judicial reasoning. Any federal power which might impinge on domestic trade or industry was to be given a restrictive or narrow interpretation in the absence of any clear indication to the contrary. In the first ten years of the Commonwealth much federal social legislation was invalidated as a result of this approach.

Both these doctrines were rather dramatically overruled in 1920 in the *Engineers Case*[25] when it was held that industrial disputes between a State and its employees could be subjected to federal industrial arbitration legislation. The method of interpretation followed was highly literalistic and legalistic, but resulted in enhanced national power. Emphasis was placed on the express terms of the Constitution and on English rules of statutory interpretation. The notion of federalism was treated as too vague and political in nature for judicial consideration. A judge's duty was simply to apply the provisions in the Act without regard to any preconceived notions, to social consequences, to possible abuses of power, or to the apparent nature of the polity created by the Constitution. These were matters for the electorate – matters of political, rather than legal concern. Federal power was to be interpreted broadly without con-

---

[25] *Amalgamated Society of Engineers v Adelaide Steamship Co. Ltd* (1920) 28 Commonwealth Law Reports 129.

sideration of what might remain in the residue. This was because the Constitution gave no express or affirmative power to the States. The correct process of interpretation was compared with that of a will, where the specific bequests are to be satisfied without regard to how much will pass to the residuary legatees.

The overthrow of the doctrines of implied State reserved powers and the subjection of the States to federal laws inevitably increased central power. It was no longer necessary to choose a limited interpretation of a Commonwealth power in order to preserve State exclusive power over certain implied subjects. The reverse was the case. As the Constitution was intended to endure for ages and was difficult to amend, the language should be interpreted broadly and generously in order to provide for unforeseen future circumstances. This principle seemed similar to that which briefly operated in relation to Canada under Lord Sankey. A former High Court judge has said that 'in 1920, the Constitution was read in a new light, a light reflected from events that had, over twenty years, led to a growing realization that Australians were now one people and Australia one country and that national laws might meet national needs.'[26] If that is so, it does not appear in the judgements, which simply purport to rely purely on rules of statutory interpretation and the express words of the Constitution.

As I mentioned, the framers considered that conferring the residue of powers on the States would ensure wider exclusive State legislative authority than was the case with Canada. The opposite has been the case. A majority of the High Court has taken the view that it is not their function to

---

[26] *Victoria v Commonwealth* (1971) 122 Commonwealth Law Reports 353, 396.

balance or weigh federal State powers because the States do not have any specified powers conferred on them. They simply have whatever is left over after a broad meaning has been given to all the federal powers. No 'federal balance' is involved. If a law can be described as one with respect to inter-State trade, taxation, immigration, banking, and so on, it is irrelevant that it might also be characterized as on some other topic. Thus a law forbidding the export of minerals mined on Fraser Island (off the coast of Queensland) was held to be within federal power with respect to overseas trade even though the purpose was not commercial but was to protect the environment of the island.[27] The law could just as easily have been described as one with respect to mining or the environment, which are not subjects of federal power, and would normally be regarded as matters for the States. Had the Constitution expressly given the States exclusive power to make laws with respect to these matters it would have been necessary for the Court (as in Canada) to make a choice. Is the law primarily or really or truly about exports or about mining or the environment? But as the Constitution reserves no topics to the States, the Court said it was unconcerned with whether it can also be described as on one of those subjects. All that is necessary is that the law can reasonably be regarded as relating to overseas trade or any other subject of federal power.

To a degree (but only to a degree) this principle has therefore avoided the situation of the Court, as in Canada, having to develop and apply distinctions and discrimen that have a high degree of political subjectivism and personal

---

[27] *Murphyores Inc. Pty Ltd v Commonwealth* (1976) 136 Commonwealth Law Reports 1.

preference. This is because any law may be regarded as being on a number of subjects.

As I have mentioned, the subject matter of the commerce power is confined to trade and commerce *with other countries and among the States*. Under the principle of implied incidental powers it is accepted that a law operating on an activity outside the subject matter (such as intra-State trade or production) may be valid if the law is reasonably necessary or appropriate to give effect to the object of the power. Thus federal control of all air navigation (including intra-State) on grounds relating to safety, regularity, and efficiency has been upheld as reasonably necessary to ensure the safety of all aircraft engaged in inter-State and overseas air navigation.[28]

Nevertheless, the Court has up to now been wary of going to the length of the United States Supreme Court, which since 1937 has regarded the control of all trading and productive processes as having a sufficient nexus with inter-State and overseas commerce because of their economic effects.[29] There is little doubt, for example, that the control of all prices or wages or the regulation of all agriculture or manufacture would not at present be regarded as a law with respect to inter-State or overseas commerce in Australia. In America, on the other hand, it is difficult to conceive of any law of an economic or commercial nature which would now be regarded as not having a sufficient connection with, or effect on, inter-State commerce.

In 1971, by a purely legal and somewhat literal approach, in the spirit of the *Engineers Case*, the Court provided the Commonwealth with a means of regulating a great deal of

---

[28] *Airlines of NSW Pty Ltd v New South Wales* [No. 2] (1965) 113 Commonwealth Law Reports 54.

[29] L. Zines, (1987) *The High Court and the Constitution* 2nd edn, chapter 4.

domestic commerce and production. Unlike what happened in America in 1936, this did not require any change in judicial approach nor the examination of economic or social data. The vehicle for achieving this result was the power to make laws with respect to 'foreign corporations and trading and financial corporations formed within the limits of the Commonwealth' (section 51(xx)). Despite the limitations on the commerce power, the Court held that, under the corporations power, the Commonwealth could control all trading and financial activities of trading and financial corporations respectively, without regard to the distinction made between the forms of trade in the commerce power. The Commonwealth has used this power to control restrictive trade practices and monopolies, to provide consumer protection, and to prohibit trade union activity calculated to damage the business of trading corporations by means of what are known in Australia as secondary boycotts.[30] In 1983 a majority of the Court held that the power extended to the control of all acts by those corporations done for the purposes of trade.[31] Three of the majority judges went further and held that the Commonwealth could control, under section 51(xx), all the acts of such corporations. Even on the more restricted view, however, the significance of these cases is that it gives the Commonwealth power to control all productive and trading activities performed by those corporations, and even though the object of the law relates to non-commercial matters. It is, however, limited to matters relating to the specified corporations. This can, from a social and economic point of view, be an arbitrary distinction.

[30] *Strickland v Rocla Concrete Pipes Ltd* (1971) 124 Commonwealth Law Reports 468; *Actors and Announcers Equity Association v Fontana Films Pty Ltd* (1982) 150 Commonwealth Law Reports 169.

[31] *Commonwealth v Tasmania* (1983) 158 Commonwealth Law Reports 1.

These developments were achieved without any public outcry or sense of amazement. However, there has been considerable criticism of the Court in recent times from many sections of the community concerning its interpretation of federal power over 'external affairs', which occurred in the *Tasmanian Dam Case*.[32] As in Canada, the Australian Government has executive capacity to enter into treaties on any subject. The States have no treaty-making capacity. However, treaties do not change domestic law. If a change in the law is required it must be done by the appropriate Parliament. By a majority of four to three, it was held that the Commonwealth Parliament had power to give effect to any international obligation under an agreement binding on Australia, no matter what its subject matter. The treaty was the World Heritage Convention and the federal law was in part aimed at preventing the Tasmanian Hydro-Electric Commission from building a dam on State land which had been placed on the World Heritage List in pursuance of that Convention. The law was, to that extent, upheld, but the Court, like the country at large, was deeply divided over the issue. Applying the approach that I have mentioned, of giving the subject a broad interpretation and ignoring the consequences for State power, it seems clear that to give legislative effect to a treaty obligation might reasonably be characterized as a law with respect to external affairs. It had been recognized for many years that power had at its core relations with other countries.

On this occasion many of the judges, rather unusually until recent times, adverted to the policy considerations involved. The dissenting minority would have limited the treaty implementation under the external affairs power to

[32] *Ibid.*

those treaties which concern the people or enterprises of other countries or which could be shown to be of sufficient international concern. They were disturbed by the notion that the Commonwealth could increase its legislative capacity by what they conceived to be a simple device of entering into a treaty. This could, in the course of time, they thought, make Australia a unitary state at the will of the federal executive.

A problem which those who support the preservation of State power have (but which is absent from Canadian constitutional arrangements) is the lack of a textual basis for deciding what exclusive powers should reside in the States. No general theory of federalism can assist in the determination of the distribution of powers between the central and regional governments. That was the basic flaw in the State reserved powers doctrine. Neither the Constitution nor federal theory gave any guidance as to which matters should be regarded as exclusively within State authority. The minority judges in the *Tasmanian Dam Case*, however, denied that they were resurrecting the notion of implied State reserved powers. They were not implying that the States had power with respect to any particular subject. Their point was that federalism required *some* area of exclusive State power.

For the majority this was not a sufficient consideration for refusing to give the external affairs power what they saw as its 'natural' meaning. It was not for the Court to consider whether a treaty had sufficient international significance. The fact that a treaty existed was enough to indicate that it had. If there was any threat to State traditional areas of authority, it was brought about, not because the founders regarded treaty implementation as inconsistent with federalism, but by the fact that more and more subjects had since then become matters of international significance and, therefore, subjects of treaties. It was not that the power had grown or changed. It was simply that the facts had changed in a manner that the framers could not have contemplated. This approach is similar to that adopted in respect of the defence power. The practical operation of the power expands or contracts in direct proportion to the external perils that the country faces. In any case, the majority said, to deny the Commonwealth this power would be to render Australia an international cripple, prevented from taking a full part in the development of world affairs and the international order.

Australia thus gained the power which had in clearer terms been granted to Canada, but which Canada was held to have lost with the gaining of international sovereignty. I should add that this power is subject to those express guarantees and restrictions which affect all federal powers, such as freedom of religion, freedom of inter-State trade, and the requirement of just terms for the acquisition of property. Also the law must be seen as an appropriate means of giving effect to the objects of the treaty. In fact two of the majority judges held invalid some provisions of the federal Act because in the view of those judges they did not satisfy this requirement, which is similar to the notion of 'proportionality' in European law.

While judicial review of legislation may be vital to a federal system, there is much more to it than that. As the British Royal Commission on the Constitution pointed out, the financial powers of the central governments in the federations appear at times to make a mockery of the formal distribution of powers. What does it matter if the central government cannot pass a law if it can coerce the regions to do so by financial threats or blandishments? This argument has been particularly common in Australia where for nearly fifty years about half of State revenues have come from Commonwealth grants. During World War II the central authorities in both Canada and Australia acquired a monopoly of income tax. In Australia this was achieved by the Commonwealth levying taxation at a rate which left little room for the States to do so, and then by making financial grants to the States on condition that they did not levy an income tax. Section 96 of the Constitution empowers the Parliament to grant financial assistance to the States on such terms and conditions as it thinks fit.

When Australian uniform tax legislation – as it was called – was upheld in 1942 it was regarded as the highwater mark of the principle of the *Engineers Case*.[33] The extent to which the judges accepted that legalistic position, involving the irrelevancy of political consequences, is clear from the comments of Latham CJ. He said that the Commonwealth could by use of these methods in practice deprive the States of all revenue-raising capacity and subject them to federal policies, thus making them administrative agents of the Commonwealth. He added that 'such a result cannot be prevented by any legal decision. The determination of the propriety of any such policy must rest with the Commonwealth Parliament and ultimately with the people.'[34]

Yet the States have not been reduced to this minor role. They remain centres of considerable real power and influence. They remain thorns in the side of the Commonwealth. It is clear that the Commonwealth cannot use its financial might to starve a State into submission for the

[33] *South Australia v Commonwealth* (1942) 65 Commonwealth Law Reports 373. See also *Victoria v Commonwealth* (1957) 99 Commonwealth Law Reports 575.
[34] 65 Commonwealth Law Reports at 429.

simple reason that the people of that State are electors in federal elections.

Yet in this sphere the different underlying political forces in Canada and Australia are interesting. The federal monopoly of income tax has continued in Australia for nearly fifty years and there is not much evident desire to change it. In Canada all the Provinces had moved back into the income tax field in one form or another by 1962. Yet the Canadian Parliament would appear to have the same power as the Commonwealth to levy tax at any rate it wishes and to make grants to the Provinces.

The federal Parliaments in both Canada and Australia also provide specific grants to the regions for particular purposes. In Australia this power has been used to procure almost complete federal control of tertiary education, even though that subject is not one conferred on the Commonwealth. The States have accepted much of this situation with equanimity. Canada also provides large amounts to the Provinces for education, but few conditions of expenditure are laid down. A similar contrasting state of affairs exists in respect of health. It is said to be politically impossible for the Canadian Government to act as the Australian Government does. As one Canadian authority has said, 'Provincial jurisdiction and control are sacrosanct'.[35]

From time to time it has been suggested that section 96 of the Australian Constitution be amended so as to prevent the Commonwealth attaching terms and conditions to the financial assistance that it gives. The purpose of such an alteration would be to prevent the Commonwealth controlling indirectly matters outside its legislative powers by means of

[35] G. Robertson,'Intergovernmental Financial Relations in Canada and Australia', in R. L. Matthews (ed.) (1982) *Public Policies in Two Federal Countries*, ANU Press, Canberra, chapter 16.

such terms and conditions to State grants. This suggestion was rejected by the Constitutional Commission on the grounds that it would not achieve its purpose.[36] The Commonwealth would, as a practical matter, remain able to extract a promise from the State as to the application of any funds granted. It could also make clear that further grants would be made only if the State acted or refrained from acting in a certain way. In other words, it is the political and social forces rather than detailed constitutional provisions which, in this area, are decisive.

Even in Australia, however, political reality prevents federal authorities from carrying out policies which are within its constitutional power. For example, the Commonwealth is very wary of using its external affairs power despite the decision in the *Tasmanian Dam Case*, because of the general concern in the community regarding that power. Therefore, despite the great increase in Australian central power, the federal spirit and federal organization run through all social institutions in Australia, from the organization of football bodies to political parties. The latter in particular, where State branches have great influence, may provide as much protection for State power as judicial review.

The great area of discretion that the broad language of constitutions leaves to the judiciary gives rise to the issue of the extent to which, first, the decisions are a reflection of underlying political and social forces and, secondly, are an influence on those forces. It is clear to me that there is a fair bit of two-way traffic. One can only speculate on what Canada or Australia would have been like if the Privy

[36] *Final Report of the Constitutional Commission* (1988) Vol. 2, 835, Australian Government Publishing Service, Canberra.

Council and the High Court had followed what was thought to have been the intention of the framers. But a study of the history of Australian and Canadian constitutional law gives force to a comment of Professor Paul Freund, made thirty-seven years ago:

[I]f the history of the federations teaches anything about the making and the life of constitutions, it is that the predictability sought from form yields to spontaneity and inventiveness in practice. In the process, a large part of which is known officially as judicial interpretation, the fate of constitutions seems to be presided over by a puckish deity of paradox.[37]

This remark is perhaps even more applicable to the European Economic Community.

Problems associated with an entrenched distribution of governmental power did not of course worry the British. The Royal Commission's report, I imagine, reflected a fairly general feeling that, in that respect, the doctrine of the sovereignty of Parliament should not be changed. In the same year as that report was issued, Britain entered the European Economic Community. There is still considerable mouthing about the sovereignty of Parliament. The reality seems otherwise. As central legislative power in Australia and, to a lesser degree, Canada has increased, the real power of Britain has diminished. If the Royal Commission could doubt whether what operated in the federations was 'true federalism', others may doubt whether any enlightenment is to be gained from regarding the British Parliament as the omnipotent legislature of a sovereign unitary state unconcerned with the distribution of powers.

It is recognized, I think, that, if the European Economic

---

[37] P. Freund, 'A Supreme Court in a Federation' (1953) 53 *Columbia Law Review* 597, 599.

Community and Britain's membership of it survives, the formal sovereignty of legislative power in Britain will be as irrelevant as that same sovereignty became to the federal systems of Canada and Australia. In strict law, in the latter countries, there were not two levels of government but three. The third was the Imperial one. Constitutional doctrine, however, evolved as if the third did not exist. Reality was adjusted to law by a strict and firm convention of abstention from the exercise of British parliamentary power.

There is always the problem of accidental breach of the Treaty, but British courts seem at times to assume (without discussion or detailed examination) that a law enacted after the coming into force of the *European Communities Act* 1972 (UK) will be inoperative if it is in breach of the Treaty or Community law. For example, in *R v Secretary of State for Transport; ex parte Factortame Ltd*[38] the House of Lords was concerned with the *Merchant Shipping Act* 1988. Lord Bridge of Harwich said that it was 'common ground' that Community rights would prevail over restrictions imposed by the latter Act.[39] Similarly in the Court of Appeal Bingham LJ declared that where the law of the Community was clear 'the duty of the national court is to give effect to it in all circumstances'. He added that 'To that extent a United Kingdom statute is no longer inviolable as it was once'. He relied on decisions of the European Court affirming the supremacy of Community law over national law.[40]

The European Economic Community is not a federal

---

[38] *R v Secretary of State for Transport; ex parte Factortame Ltd* [1989] 2 Weekly Law Reports 997.

[39] *Ibid.*, 1011.

[40] *R v Secretary of State for Transport; ex parte Factortame Ltd* [1989] 2 Common Market Law Reports 353, 403, 404.

FEDERAL AND SUPRA-NATIONAL FEATURES

state. It has been variously described as 'supra-national', 'a variant of federalism', 'functional federalism', 'an association of sovereign states with federal potential', and as 'having characteristics of both federal governments and international functional organizations'.

The student of federalism is struck by the similarity of many of the problems, issues, and arguments before the European Court with those that have been faced by courts in Canada, Australia, and the United States. The most fundamental and vital decisions of the Court which made relevant the analogy of federalism were those that held provisions of the Treaty and Community law could have direct effect within the national systems. Independently of state legislation, they could confer benefits and impose duties on individuals.[41] In other words, the Court rejected the argument that the treaty was merely an international agreement, and treated it as the framework of government of a polity in which powers were divided between the centre and the regions.

Upon this foundation the Court brought into play many principles and doctrines that are familiar in the constitutional law of the federations. Many of the issues that the European Court has had to resolve are the same as, or remarkably similar to, those that have been examined or applied in the courts of Australia, Canada, and the United States.

These include such questions and issues as:

(a) the reserve powers of the states;
(b) when central legislation covers the field so as to exclude

[41] *Van Gend en Loos v Nederlandse Administratie Der Belastingen* [1963] European Court Reports 1, 12; *Costa v ENEL* (1964) European Court Reports 585.

or pre-empt all state law in the area, so making concurrent powers exclusive;
(c) when a provision not directly within power may be regarded as incidental to the power or necessary or proper to achieve some purpose within power;
(d) whether any powers are to be implied from the very nature of the Community;
(e) the extent to which notions of civil liberty are relevant to the validity of Community provisions; and
(f) whether provisions relating to the free movement of goods are aimed only at laws which are protectionist or reduce the total volume of trade or whether they permit the individual to ignore rules that prevent *him* from trading, whatever the effect on general trade.[42]

All these matters have been examined by one or more of the courts of the federations to which I have referred.

Yet the European Court seems to me to have manifested a degree of boldness, daring, and commitment to a cause that surpasses that of the highest courts in the federations. For this it has secured praise and has had bitter criticism heaped upon it. It is probable that much of this so-called teleological approach (based, as Justice Pescatore has said, on 'an idea of Europe' held by the judges, but not shared by all others[43]) has been due to those features of the EEC which differ from the federations.

The most important of these features are, first, that the Treaty is really a dynamic programme intended to move towards what the preamble calls 'ever closer union among

[42] See, generally, L. Zines, 'The Balancing of Community and National Interests by the European Court' (1973) 5 *Federal Law Review* 171, 174.
[43] Pescatore, 'The Doctrine of Direct Effect: An Infant Disease of Community Law' (1983) 8 *European Law Review* 155.

the peoples of Europe'. Whereas central powers in Canada and Australia are in the form of subject matters, leaving the policy to be pursued within those areas to the political process, the Community's powers are usually not to make laws or to take measures *about subjects*, but to make them *for objects*, i.e. to achieve particular goals. The Community therefore involves not merely a transfer of sovereignty, but a commitment to certain policies. This lack of legislative discretion, however, should not be exaggerated. Many of the objectives are very broad and in a practical sense may be contradictory. Various objects of the agricultural policy set out in article 39, for example, need balancing and compromise because they concern conflicting interests, such as the objective in paragraph (b) to increase the earnings of persons engaged in agriculture, and that in paragraph (e) to ensure that supplies reach consumers at reasonable prices.

It can generally be said that entry into the Community, like entry into a federation, does involve the surrender of power from the regions to the centre; but there are some matters that were, for example, in the competence of Westminster before entering the Community that cannot now be enacted by the British Parliament *or* the Community authorities either jointly or severally. One example would be the encouragement of cartels.

The second non-federal factor that has been of great significance is that from a Community view the weakest organ of government is the legislature – the Council – which is comprised of state ministers. Among the institutions of the Community, this body resembles in practice an intergovernmental diplomatic assembly rather than a Community institution. It is of course the Council rather than the elected Parliament that is the effective law-maker. The Treaty has endeavoured to counteract the obvious centrifugal influences in the Council by often requiring measures to be taken only on a proposal of the Commission and requiring unanimity to override the Commission. The Single European Act provides for more decisions to be made by a qualified majority of the Council, and it will to a degree also strengthen the influence and position of the elected Parliament. But even so, it is clear that the nature of the Council is such that it cannot always be relied on to protect the objects, interests, and institutional authority of the Community against state interests and pressures. The members making up the Council are not responsible to the body which is elected by the people of Europe, but to their own legislatures.

It appears that the European Court has seen it as its duty to further Community goals when they have languished amid the clash of policies and the self-interest of the nation-states, which are proportionately more powerful than the members of any federation. There is no doubt that the Court has acted as the greatest centralizing force in the Community, expanding Community powers and restricting state powers in a manner that would not have occurred if matters had been left for determination in the Council.

Indeed, because of state influence in the Council the Court has sometimes felt obliged to protect Community values against Council, or even Commission, policies by invalidating regulations or directions made by them, where they would have weakened or undermined Common Market policies.[44]

It is true that in Australia, also, federal laws may be invalid because of interference with the freedom of inter-

[44] *Wine Levy* [1978] European Court Reports 927; *Bock v Commission* [1971] European Court Reports 897; *Kaufhof v Commission* [1976] European Court Reports 431.

State trade. This is because section 92 of the Constitution provides that 'trade, commerce and intercourse among the States shall be absolutely free'. This provision binds both the Commonwealth and the States.[45] But its scope is more limited than the Treaty of Rome and, under current doctrine, it is not much of a barrier to the implementation of federal policies approved by Parliament.[46]

It is not possible, in the course of a lecture, to illustrate the matters I have mentioned in respect of the many areas of Community law that have been developed by the European Court. An examination of the subject of external affairs, however, encapsulates (1) the position of the Court, the Commission, and the Council, (2) the judicial method which has been the Court's hallmark, and (3) some of the effects of EEC membership on the powers of the Crown and Parliament of the United Kingdom.

In 1962 an international agreement prepared under the auspices of an international body was signed by some members of the EEC. It concerned the work of crews of vehicles in international road transport. The agreement never came into force because of insufficient ratifications. Community regulations by the Council were enacted to regulate the matter.

Steps were then taken to revise the earlier agreement to enable more states to become parties to it. The members of the Council discussed what attitude their respective states would take at the negotiations. Those negotiations were successfully concluded by the states in accordance with the discussion, and a draft agreement was open for signature by them. Before the states who were members of the EEC could

[45] *James v Commonwealth* (1936) 55 Commonwealth Law Reports 1.
[46] *Cole v Whitfield* (1988) 78 Australian Law Reports 42.

sign, however, the Community regulations needed amending. They could be amended by the Council only on a proposal of the Commission. The Commission was asked to come up with the appropriate proposal. It refused to do so and instead commenced an action to annul the Council's discussion, regarding the negotiations, and the conclusion of the agreement by the states.

Although, because of special circumstances, the Court found in favour of the Council, it held that in principle the negotiation of the agreement was a matter for the Community, not for the states. Under article 228 the agreement was required to be negotiated by the Commission and concluded by the Council.[47]

The approach of the Court can be discerned by looking to see what textual apparatus the Court had with which to work. The Treaty of Rome makes express provision for Community treaties in two areas only; namely, commercial agreements (articles 111–16) and agreements of association with third states (article 238). There is no express power in relation to transport or any other subject. In respect of transport the Treaty merely provides, so far as is relevant, that the objectives shall be pursued by member states within the framework of a common transport policy and that the Council for that purpose may lay down common rules, conditions applicable to non-residents, and 'any other appropriate provisions'.

The Advocate-General (an independent and impartial officer) strongly argued that the Court should hold that the Community did not have power in this respect. The Community, he said, only had those powers expressly conferred

[47] *Re. European Road Transport Agreement: E C Commission v E C Council* [1971] European Court Reports 263.

on it. It appeared from the Treaty that the authors intended strictly to limit the Community's authority in external matters to the cases which they expressly laid down. He said that to conclude that the Community had treaty-making capacity in that case would 'involve you in creating new law in the manner of the Roman Praetor'.

The Court decided that the role of Praetor fitted it very well. It held that the Community had capacity to enter into international agreements over 'the whole extent of the field of the objectives defined in Part One of the Treaty'. The particular objective concerned was a common policy on transport. This argument was buttressed by article 210 of the Treaty, which declared that 'The Community shall have a legal personality'.

Accepting that the Community had power, why was it not concurrent? The Court said:

Each time the Community, with a view to implementing a common policy envisaged by the Treaty, lays down common rules, whatever form these may take, the member states no longer have the right to act individually or collectively to incur obligations toward non-member states affecting those rules.[48]

This view was confirmed in 1976 in the *Kramer* case[49] relating to the preservation and conservation of fish. The Court held that the Community had general power to enter into international commitments in this area. On this occasion there was still a transitional period and the Dutch could therefore at that time have temporary authority, but the Netherlands had a duty to ensure that the Community's task was not made more difficult.

In these cases the Court appeared to limit its holding to

[48] *Ibid.* 274.
[49] [1976] European Court Reports 1279.

instances where the Community had legislated in the area. The Advocate-General, in addressing that question, in the first case, had argued that such a view would hamper the development of Community law and common policies, because there were grounds for fearing that the ministers would resist the adoption of regulations which would result in the loss of their authority in international matters.

In 1977 the Court avoided this problem by going further. It declared that the Community had power to make international agreements to attain any specific object of the Community even where the Community had no internal rules, and the subject was still governed by state laws. Again the reasons were general or 'teleological' and rested on no specific provisions. The Court said:

> [T]he power to bind the Community *vis-à-vis* third countries ... flows by implication from the provisions of the Treaty creating the internal power and in so far as the participation of the Community in the international agreement is, as here, necessary for the attainment of one of the objectives of the Community.[50]

State members were permitted also to be parties to the agreement in that case, which related to traffic on inland waterways, so that certain obstacles relating to pre-EEC conventions could be removed. The Court emphasized that limited purpose and declared that for all other purposes the legal effects of the agreement resulted solely from its conclusion by the Community.

This particular series of cases underlines a number of features of the Community system and operation.

First, the extent to which the Community differs from a

[50] *Opinion given pursuant to Article 288(i) of the EEC Treaty* [1977] European Court Reports 741, 755.

federation may be gauged from the attitudes of the parties to the first case. The chief legislative organ of the Community was strenuously arguing that it did not have power to deal with the matter and that it belonged to the states. The bureaucracy, an independent organ, took the reverse position.

Secondly, the Court's approach was to emphasize heavily the general aims of the Community in order to extend central power. It showed little concern with the detailed provisions, which might have been thought to confine the Community's power over external relations to the matters mentioned. It shows (and there are many other areas where the same attitude is evident) that the tendency is often to examine only if the end is desirable and then to ask whether the presence of a Community power or the ousting of state power would be an appropriate means to that end.

Thirdly, it follows from the cases that there is taken from the British Crown a considerable and widening portion of its prerogative power to enter into treaties and from the power of the British Parliament to legislate on the subject matter of treaties. Another fundamental rule of the British Constitution is also affected. Whereas a Crown treaty cannot, generally speaking, alter the law of the land, a Community treaty that is self-executing can have a direct effect, and so confer rights and impose duties on individuals.[51]

Where the treaty specifically refers to powers of the states to deal with subjects which may impinge on the common market, such as morality, safety, or health (as in, for example, article 36), the Court declared that these are

[51] *International Fruit Co.* [1972] European Court Reports 1219; *Kupferberg* [1982] European Court Reports 361.

exceptions that must therefore be interpreted strictly.[52] This approach is similar to that applied to State legislation in Australia and the United States which derogates from the freedom of inter-state trade. The Courts in both countries have held that the measures taken to protect the local interest should not be greater than is reasonably necessary and appropriate for the purpose, having regard to the need to protect the freedom of inter-State trade.[53] The European Court, however, in applying this principle of proportionality, seems to have been less liberal in upholding the non-protectionist legislation of the states.

Issues have arisen as to environmental and consumer protection which have caused debate as to whether the Community is to be seen as primarily a mercantilist union or as something broader. In the past decade or so Community law in these areas in the form of regulations and of directives to harmonize laws have increased considerably.

Article 100 of the Treaty empowers the Council, unanimously, to issue directives for broadly uniform laws on matters that 'directly affect the establishment or functioning of the Common Market'. It has been said in the British Parliament that whenever it enacts a law in pursuance of such a directive the Parliament loses power 'down a one-way street'. Concern was expressed by some members that directives about social matters like consumer protection etc. were not the concern of the Community and therefore not within

---

[52] *Simmenthal* [1978] European Court Reports 629; *Denkavit* [1979] European Court Reports 3369; *Commission v Belgium* [1983] European Court Reports 531.
[53] *North Eastern Dairy Co. Ltd v Dairy Industry Authority of New South Wales* (1975) 134 Commonwealth Law Reports 559; *Dean Milk Co. v City of Madison* (1951) 340 United States Reports 349; *Minnesota v Clover Leaf Creamery Co.* (1981) 449 United States Reports 456.

article 100.[54] Similar concern has been expressed regarding use of article 235 of the Treaty which provides 'If action by the Community should prove necessary to attain, *in the course of the operation of the common market,* one of the objectives of the Community and this Treaty has not provided the necessary powers, the Council shall, acting unanimously on a proposal of the Commission and after consulting the Assembly, take the appropriate measures' (emphasis supplied).[55]

It may be that this pressure by the member states themselves to widen central control in areas such as environmental and consumer protection derives directly from the strict limitations applied by the Court on state powers to deal with non-commercial subjects that impinge upon interstate trade. The danger is that standards of protection under state laws in areas of health, safety, the environment, and so on may be required to be minimal. This can best be overcome by central or common rules. This to a degree has been recognized by the states approving in Council rules and directives with social objects that impinge on the market.

There may, however, be a more economic motive with which federal communities are familiar. The co-operation of the states in greater Community control and harmonization may come about because, given the commitment to the freedom of inter-State trade, local attempts to have high standards of, for example, quality, health, or environmental control may be self-defeating. This is because they have to

[54] G. Close, 'Harmonisation of Laws: use or abuse of the powers under the EEC Treaty?' (1978) 3 *European Law Review* 461.
[55] C. Sasse and H. C. Yaurow, 'The Growth of Legislative Power of the European Communities', in T. Sandalow and E. Stein, *Courts and Free Markets: Perspectives from the United States and Europe* (1982), Vol. 1, Clarendon Press, Oxford; Oxford University Press, New York, 96 et seq.

meet competition from states that have less costly standards. The import of foreign goods and the export of capital can threaten unilateral state attempts to regulate a particular subject.[56] The Court therefore may have indirectly created a situation whereby the states themselves, to a degree, are contributing to the expansion of central power.[57]

It might be added that there are signs that the Court may be adopting a more flexible approach to state laws in these areas and a more deliberate weighing of Community and state interests.[58] Also, the Single European Act has amended the Treaty by inserting a new title relating to the environment (Title VII) and new provisions concerning state laws relating to the environment and the working environment. On other social questions Britain and many of the other states are divided.

It is clear that Britain now finds itself concerned with problems of the distribution of legislative and executive powers. Although not a member of a federation and still clinging to the doctrine of parliamentary sovereignty, the position of Britain in relation to the Community strikes the outside observer as having marked similarity, in that respect, to the federations that Britain created.

---

[56] T. Heller, 'Legal Theory and Political Economy of American Federation, in M. Cappeletti, M. Segcombe, and J. Weiler (eds.), *Integration Through Law: Europe and the American Federal Experience* (1985), Vol. 1, Book 1, W. De Gruyter, Berlin, 273.
[57] G. Close, 'Harmonisation of Laws: use or abuse of the powers under the EEC Treaty?' (1978) 3 *European Law Review* 461.
[58] *Amsterdam Bulb* [(1977] European Court Reports 137.

INDEX

Air Navigation
 Canadian federal power, 82, 84
Australian Acts, 21–2
 'peace, order, and good government' of state, 48
Australian Constitution
 amendment, 23–4
 banning of Communist Party, 40
 central power increased from 1920, 89 *et seq*
 constitutional rights, 60
 corporations power, 91–2
 demarcation of powers, 78–9
 employment law, 88
 environment; federal power over, 90, 93–5
 external affairs power, 18–20, 93–5
 federal powers; method of interpretation, 90–1
 federalism as factor in interpreting, 87, 93–5
 financial assistance to States, 97–8
 freedom of interstate trade; compared with EEC, 104–5, 110
 freedom of speech, 40–1
 human rights and interpretation of powers, 39–41, 42
 implied rights, 45–6, 50
 income tax; federal monopoly, 95–6
 inconsistency of federal and State laws, 42
 intergovernmental relations, 87 *et seq*
 interpretation contrasted with Canadian, 89–91
 interpretation of rights, 62–5
 parliamentry power to override proposed rights, 60–2
 political forces sustaining federalism, 96–8
 power to remove State colonial restrictions, 18 *et seq*
 present legal basis for, 25–8
 Privy Council; limited jurisdiction, 86–7
 production; federal control of, 92
 proposed amendments to entrench rights, 60–3
 rejection of Canadian model, 78
 reserved powers of States, 87 *et seq*
 restrictive trade practices; federal control, 92
 retention of colonial relics, 23–4
 royal succession, 29–31
 trade and commerce power, 90–1
 US influence, 87
 war and external affairs, 6
Australian Constitutional Commission
 recommended constitutional rights, 60–3

113

INDEX

Australian Government
advice to Queen re State request, 16–17
relationship with UK, 10,11
Australian States
appointment of Governor, 2
attitude to Statue of Westminster, 7–9
comparison with Canadian Provinces, 8
constitutional links with the UK, 8, 10
consultation with; by UK Government, 17–18
effect of Imperial legislation, 2
effect of Statue of Westminster, 10
methods of abolishing colonial restrictions, 15 *et seq*
no separation of powers, 49
removing colonial restrictions by federal legislation, 18 *et seq*
reserved powers, 87 *et seq*, 93–5
rights implied by in State Constitution, 48–50, 51
royal succession, 30–1

Balfour Declaration, 1
Bill of Rights
attempts to enact in UK, 39
Canadian; interpretation of, 65–6
New Zealand draft. See *New Zealand Draft Bill of Rights*
US; *laissez-faire* interpretation, 52–3
British Empire and Commonwealth
Crown prerogatives, 3–4
law and conventions of, 2 *et seq*
British Government
advice to Queen re State request 16–17
defendant before European Court on Human Rights, 38–9
British North American Act
see *Canadian Constitution*
British Parliament
amendment of Canadian Constitution, 12 *et seq*
no power over Canada, Australia, or New Zealand, 24–5
omnipotence in Canada before 1982, 14
power limited by treaties entered into by EEC, 109
reconciliation of sovereignty with EEC, 100

Canada Act, 14–15
Canadian Charter of Rights and Freedoms
categories of rights, 55
citizenship as requirement for admission as lawyer, 70–1
criminal justice protections, 67
enactment, 15
equality, 56, 70–1
evidence of social facts, 57–8
'free and democratic society'; onus on Government to show necessity of law, 57
freedom of association; right to strike, 67–8
interpretation, 66–71
'life, liberty, and security'; anti-abortion laws, 68
limitation on rights, 57
Parliamentry power to override, 58–9
'principles of fundamental justice', 56, 68–70
Canadian Constitution
abolition of Privy Council appeals, 4–5
air navigation, 82, 84
amendment by UK Parliament, 2, 12, *et seq*
centralized system intended, 77–8
contrast with Australian, 78–9
demarcatoin of powers, 77–8
emergencies, 81
inflation and unemployment, 84
federal balance, 84–6
federal residuary power, 77, 81, 82
off-shore resources, 84
financial assistance to Provinces, 97–8
human rights and interpretation of

114

INDEX

powers, 41
implied rights, 43–5
interpretation contrasted with Australian, 89–91
interpretation of rights before Charter, 65–6
'living tree' doctrine, 81–2
political forces sustaining federalism, 96–8
'property and civil rights', 79 *et seq*
present legal basis for, 25–8
restrictive trade practices; control of 85–6
royal succession, 29
search for amending formula, 12–13
see also *Canadian Charter of Rights and Freedoms*
terms of employment, 82–3
trade and commerce power, 80 *et seq*
expansion of, 85–6
treaty implementation, 82, 83
'watertight compartments' doctrine, 83

Canadian Parliament
power to request UK of amendment of Constitution, 14

Canadian Provinces
application of Statue of Westminster to, 10
comparison with Australian States, 8
consultation with; by UK Government, 17–18
power over economic activity, 80, 86

Common Law
as limitation on parliamentry supremacy, 47–8, 51
not fully protective of human rights, 38–9, 73

Constitutional Conventions
advice to Queen by British and Australian Governments, 16–17
Canadian Constitution amendment, 12, 14
led to Dominion independence, 5–6

Constitutional Interpretation
ability of courts to interpret rights, 62–7
affected by political and social forces, 98–9
Canadian and Australian contrasted, 89–91
Canadian and US contrasted, 82
Canadian criticism of Privy Council, 83–4
Canadian federal balance, 84–6
effect on, of independance from UK, 28
federalism as a factor in, 87, 93–5
human rights as a factor, 39 *et seq*
in EEC, compared with federal constitutions, 101 *et seq*
literal; in Australia, 88–9
produces greater central power in Australia, 92
results different from founders intentions, 79

Constitutional Rights
ability of courts to interpret, 62–7
British attitudes to, 33–4
criticism of judges implying, 52–4
democracy, 34–5
implied, 43 *et seq*
New Zealand Draft Bill of Rights, 59–60
proposed amendments to Australian constitution, 60–3
see also *Bill of Rights*
see also *Canadian Charter of Rights and Freedoms*

Consumer Protection
in the EEC

Court of the European Communities
see *European Court*

Courts
ability to interpret constitutional rights, 62–7
control of administration and executive, 35–7, 62

Crown
advice to; by Dominion authorities, 3
EEC limits treaty power, 109
indivisibility in Empire, 3
royal succession law, 28–31

INDEX

in Australia, 29–31
in Canada, 29
in New Zealand, 29
same Queen, but different Crowns, 31–2

Democracy
flaws in, 34–5
relationship to constitutional rights, 34–5

Dominion Constitutions
based on Imperial enactment, 3
interpretation affected by political status, 4–5, 6

Dominions
advice to Crown, 3
effect of British declaration of war on, 1–2, 5
evolution to independence, 1

Employment Law
Australian constitution, 88, 91
Canadian constitution, 82–3

Environment
EEC power over, 110–13
federal power over; in Australia, 90
implementation of treaties in Australia, 93–5

European Convention on Human Rights
as standard of rights in UK, 71–2
British early concerns about, 53–4
limitations on rights, 56–7
practical check on UK power, 54
UK as a party to, 37–9

European Court
forces States to expand central power, 110–13
greatest centralizing force in EEC, 103 *et seq*
methods of interpretation, 101 *et seq*
teleological method of interpretation, 102, 109

European Court of Human Rights
Britons may petition, 37–8
UK as defendant, 38–9

European Economic Community
Commission check on centrifugal forces in Council, 103–4, 109
Commission upholding Community powers, 109
Community law may have direct effect, 101
compared with federal state, 100 *et seq*
contrasted with federal state, 102–5, 108–9
Council compared with diplomatic assembly, 102–4
Court is greatest centralizing force, 103 *et seq*
dynamic programme, 102–3
external affairs powers of, 105–10
freedom of interstate trade;
compared with Australia, 104–5
compared with Australia and the US, 110
harmonization of laws, 110
power over social issues, 110–12
state power to impinge on Common Market, 109–10
transport laws, 105–7
UK laws inconsistent with, 100

Federalism
as factor in interpreting Australian Constitution, 87
as factor in interpreting Australian treaty power, 93–5
coercion of regions by financial means, 95–6
compared with EEC, 100 *et seq*
contrasted with EEC, 102–5
distinguished from UK, 76–7
human rights as factor in constitutional interpretation, 39 *et seq*
political forces sustaining, 96–8
political forces in Canada and Australia contrasted, 96–8
UK attitudes to, 75–6

Governor
imperial and local officer, 3–4
none in Western Australia, 1933–1947, 19

116

INDEX

Governor-General
appointment on local advice, 6

Income and Prices
Canadian power to control, 84
Intergovernmental Relations
Australia, 87 *et seq*

Kershaw Committee
amendment of Canadian Constitution, 13, 14–15, 17–18

New Zealand
implied rights, 47–8, 54
New Zealand Constitution
abolition of upper house, 23
ouster of UK power, 23
present legal basis for, 25–8
repeal of Statue of Westminster, 23
royal succession, 29
sovereign Parliament, 23
New Zealand Draft Bill of Rights
contents, 59–60
recommendation that it not be entrenched, 72

Parliament
Executive power over, 35
see also *Supremacy of Parliament*
People
as basis for Constitutions, 27–8
Perogatives
operating throughout Empire, 3–4
treaty; limited in UK by EEC, 109
Privy Council
abolition of Australian appeals, 22
abolition of Canadian appeals, 4–5, 83
appeals from Australia, 11
Canadian criticism of, 83–4
interpretation of Canadian Constitution, 79
limited jurisdiction in Australia, 86–7
refusal to refer Australian State request for advice to, 16–17

Quebec
attitude to constitutional amendment, 14
Queen
advice to; on State matters, 22
as head of several independent countries, 31–2
conflicting advice from Australian Federal and State Governments, 15–17

Restrictive Trade Practices
Australian control of, 92
Canadian control of, 85–6
Royal Commission on UK Constitution, 75–6
Rule of Law
in constitutional interpretation, 40

Statute of Westminster, 1
adoption by Australia and New Zealand, 7
attitude of Australia and New Zealand to, 7
effect on UK Parliaments' power, 26
extra-territorial legislation, 5
New Zealand repeal, 23
power to override Imperial law, 5
repeal of s 4 in Australia, 22
safeguards for Australian States, 9
Supremacy of Parliament
Canadian Charter; compromise, 58
common law limitation, 47–8, 50
constitutional rights, 34–5
judicial review of administration; practical check on, 62
overriding of entrenched rights
  Australia, 60–2
  Canada, 58–9
  New Zeland, 59
UK parliamentary sovereignty and EEC, 99–100

Taxation
federal monopoly of income tax in Australia and Canada, 95–6

INDEX

Transport
  EEC laws controlling, 105–7
Treaties
  Australian power to implement, 93–5
  Canadian and Australian power contrasted, 95
  Canadian power to implement, 82, 83
  entered into by EEC may change law, 109
  negotiation and implementation in EEC, 105–10
  UK treaty power reduced by EEC, 109
Treaty of Rome
  interpreted like a federal constitution, 101–2

see also *European Economic Community*

United States Constitution
  bill of rights; *laissez-faire* interpretation, 52–3
  commerce power; contrasted with Australian, 91
  expansion of national power from 1937, 82
  freedom of interstate trade; compared with EEC, 110
  influence on form of Australian Constitution, 87

Western Australia
  attempt at secession, 9
  no Governor from 1933–47, 19